# MACMILLAN MASTER GUIDES

General Edi...
Published :

JANE AUSTEN: PRIDE AND PREJUDICE Raym...
    EMMA Norm... ...ge
    MANSFIELD PARK Richard Wirdn...

ROBERT BOLT: A MAN FOR ALL SEASONS Leonard Smith

EMILY BRONTË: WUTHERING HEIGHTS Hilda D. Spear

GEOFFREY CHAUCER: THE PROLOGUE TO THE CANTERBURY TALES
    Nigel Thomas and Richard Swan
    THE MILLER'S TALE Michael Alexander

CHARLES DICKENS: BLEAK HOUSE Dennis Butts
    GREAT EXPECTATIONS Dennis Butts
    HARD TIMES Norman Page

GEORGE ELIOT: MIDDLEMARCH Graham Handley
    SILAS MARNER Graham Handley

E. M. FORSTER: A PASSAGE TO INDIA Hilda D. Spear

THE METAPHYSICAL POETS Joan van Emden

WILLIAM GOLDING: LORD OF THE FLIES Raymond Wilson

OLIVER GOLDSMITH: SHE STOOPS TO CONQUER Paul Ranger

THOMAS HARDY: FAR FROM THE MADDING CROWD Colin Temblett-Wood
    TESS OF THE D'URBERVILLES James Gibson

CHRISTOPHER MARLOWE: DOCTOR FAUSTUS David A. Male

ARTHUR MILLER: THE CRUCIBLE Leonard Smith

GEORGE ORWELL: ANIMAL FARM Jean Armstrong

WILLIAM SHAKESPEARE: MACBETH David Elloway
    A MIDSUMMER NIGHT'S DREAM Kenneth Pickering
    ROMEO AND JULIET Helen Morris
    THE WINTER'S TALE Diana Devlin
    HENRY IV PART I Helen Morris

GEORGE BERNARD SHAW: ST JOAN Leonée Ormond

RICHARD SHERIDAN: THE RIVALS Jeremy Rowe
    THE SCHOOL FOR SCANDAL Paul Ranger

Forthcoming:

SAMUEL BECKETT: WAITING FOR GODOT J. Birkett

WILLIAM BLAKE: SONGS OF INNOCENCE AND SONGS OF EXPERIENCE
    A. Tomlinson

GEORGE ELIOT: THE MILL ON THE FLOSS H. Wheeler

T. S. ELIOT: MURDER IN THE CATHEDRAL P. Lapworth

HENRY FIELDING: JOSEPH ANDREWS T. Johnson

E. M. FORSTER: HOWARD'S END I. Milligan

WILLIAM GOLDING: THE SPIRE R. Sumner

THOMAS HARDY: THE MAYOR OF CASTERBRIDGE R. Evans

SELECTED POEMS OF GERALD MANLEY HOPKINS

PHILIP LARKIN: THE WHITSUN WEDDING AND THE LESS DECEIVED
    A. Swarbrick

D. H. LAWRENCE: SONS AND LOVERS R. Draper

HARPER LEE: TO KILL A MOCKINGBIRD Jean Armstrong

THOMAS MIDDLETON: THE CHANGELING A. Bromham

ARTHUR MILLER: DEATH OF A SALESMAN P. Spalding

WILLIAM SHAKESPEARE: HAMLET J. Brooks
    HENRY V P. Davison
    KING LEAR F. Casey
    JULIUS CAESAR David Elloway
    MEASURE FOR MEASURE M. Lilly
    OTHELLO Christopher Beddows
    RICHARD II C. Barber
    TWELFTH NIGHT Edward Leeson
    THE TEMPEST Kenneth Pickering

TWO PLAYS OF JOHN WEBSTER David A. Male

*Also published by Macmillan*

**MASTERING ENGLISH LITERATURE** R. Gill
**MASTERING ENGLISH LANGUAGE** S. H. Burton
**MASTERING ENGLISH GRAMMAR** S. H. Burton

## WORK OUT SERIES

**WORK OUT ENGLISH LANGUAGE** ('O' level and GCSE) S. H. Burton
**WORK OUT ENGLISH LITERATURE** ('A' level) S. H. Burton

# MACMILLAN MASTER GUIDES
# THE SCHOOL FOR SCANDAL
# BY RICHARD SHERIDAN

PAUL RANGER

**MACMILLAN**

First edition 1986

Published by
MACMILLAN EDUCATION LTD
Houndmills, Basingstoke, Hampshire RG21 2XS
and London
Companies and representatives
throughout the world

Typeset by
TecSet Ltd., Sutton, Surrey

Printed in Hong Kong

ISBN 0-333-39979-X  Pbk
ISBN 0-333-39980-3  Pbk export

# CONTENTS

# GENERAL EDITOR'S PREFACE

The aim of the Macmillan Master Guides is to help you to appreciate the book you are studying by providing information about it and by suggesting ways of reading and thinking about it which will lead to a fuller understanding. The section on the writer's life and background has been designed to illustrate those aspects of the writer's life which have influenced the work, and to place it in its personal and literary context. The summaries and critical commentary are of special importance in that each brief summary of the action is followed by an examination of the significant critical points. The space which might have been given to repetitive explanatory notes has been devoted to a detailed analysis of the kind of passage which might confront you in an examination. Literary criticism is concerned with both the broader aspects of the work being studied and with its detail. The ideas which meet us in reading a great work of literature, and their relevance to us today, are an essential part of our study, and our Guides look at the thought of their subject in some detail. But just as essential is the craft with which the writer has constructed his work of art, and this is considered under several technical headings - characterisation, language, style and stagecraft.

The authors of these Guides are all teachers and writers of wide experience, and they have chosen to write about books they admire and know well in the belief that they can communicate their admiration to you. But you yourself must read and know intimately the book you are studying. No one can do that for you. You should see this book as a lamppost. Use it to shed light, not to lean against. If you know your text and know what it is saying about life, and how it says it, then you will enjoy it, and there is no better way of passing an examination in literature.

JAMES GIBSON

# ACKNOWLEDGEMENTS

Cover illustration: *The Explanation*, An Engraving by H. Humphrey. © Bridgeman Art Library.

# 1 RICHARD BRINSLEY SHERIDAN AND THE BACKGROUND TO THE PLAY

## 1.1 PLAYWRIGHT, MANAGER AND POLITICIAN

**The playwright**

Richard Brinsley Sheridan enjoyed three careers: he was a playwright, a theatre manager and a politician.

He originated from a noted Irish family, the O'Sheridans. After an education at Harrow School he went to live in Bath where his father, Thomas Sheridan (1721-88), an erstwhile theatre manager, gave ponderous lectures on elocution, enlivened with songs sung by an attractive Miss Elizabeth Linley (1754-92). Elizabeth's beauty made her the toast of Bath. The playwright Samuel Foote (1720-77) wrote an entertaining comedy about an elderly gentleman's proposal of marriage to this young lady, and his subsequent retraction, under the title *The Maid of Bath*. The young Sheridan fell in love with her and, discovering that she was hounded by a dishonourable suitor named Thomas Matthews, eloped with her to France. Miss Linley's father persuaded the couple to return to England and they were married at Marylebone Church in 1773.

In order to support his wife, who was not without money, Sheridan began work on his first play *The Rivals*, and which contained elements of autobiography; before his marriage Sheridan had fought two duels with Matthews, in one of which he was seriously wounded, and it was these which prompted the amusing duel scene in the last act of the play. It was set in Bath, a city Sheridan knew, and it reflects the daily events of that fashionable spa. After a false start and a rewrite the comedy was enthusiastically received in January 1775 at the Theatre Royal, Covent Garden. Sheridan's literary career had begun.

Several comedies rapidly followed at the rival playhouse, the Theatre Royal, Drury Lane, and in May 1777 *The School for Scandal* was given in this theatre. Instantly the comedy received the accolade of success. In 1781 Sheridan wrote a light-hearted judgement of the current foibles of the stage in *The Critic*. In this he marked such conventions as the sentimental heroine, the recognition of long-lost relatives, and patriotic spectacle.

A gap of eighteen years separated *The Critic* from Sheridan's final play, *Pizarro*, a tragedy in which the perversity of the cruel Spanish *conquistadors* is contrasted with the natural goodness of the Peruvian people. Sentiment runs riot in this play; and the second act, set in the Inca Temple of the Sun, is an opportunity for elaborate spectacle and rousing calls for the defence of one's native land, which found echoes in the hearts of Englishmen as they prepared to defend the south coast against the threatened encroachments of Napoleon's forces.

### The theatre manager

The financial success of Sheridan's early comedies prompted him to become interested in the management of the Theatre Royal, Drury Lane. Since 1747 the theatre had been administered by the actor David Garrick (1717-79) and it was from him that Sheridan purchased a substantial share of the management in 1776. In the previous year was completed a thorough restoration of the one-hundred-year-old building by the architect Robert Adam (1728-92). The theatre had been considered drab and pokey. To lighten it Adam painted the interior in shades of green and pink, and set up mirrors and lustres to make the auditorium appear more spacious. An audience numbering 1800 could be crammed within the walls of the theatre.

Sheridan realised that if his theatre was to pay handsome dividends the auditorium would have to be enlarged; and in order to pander to the public demand for spectacular entertainments the stage area would require redesigning. The demolition of the building he had bought from Garrick began in 1791, and three years later a new theatre, designed by Henry Holland (1745-1806), was opened. It boasted the largest stage in Europe. Sarah Siddons (1755-1831), one of the greatest performers on the Georgian stage, referred to the theatre as 'this vast wilderness'. It was, for it held nearly 4000 spectators.

Fire in a theatre lit by candles and oil lamps was an ever-present danger. Londoners lined the banks of the Thames in 1809 to watch the Theatre Royal, Drury Lane, burn to a shell. A financially ruined Sheridan sat in a hostelry opposite, much moved by the sight of his own theatre in flames. When friends pressed him to return home, he remarked, 'May not a man take a glass of wine by his own fireside?' But it was his own no longer, and a syndicate was formed to administer the new playhouse which rose from the ashes.

### The politician

Sheridan was elected to the House of Commons in 1780 and remained there for the next thirty years. The government was led by William Pitt the Younger (1759-1806), and, as a member of the Whig party, Sheridan was a vociferous opponent of that Tory gentleman's policies. Fearful that Englishmen would emulate the French in the Revolution of 1789 and rise against monarchy and government, Pitt suspended the Habeas Corpus Act which legislated against imprisonment without trial, placed limitations on the Press, harshly punished critics of his government, and strongly resisted the abolition of the slave trade. Sheridan was a staunch supporter of the efforts of William Wilberforce (1759-1833) to stop the practice of enslaving native peoples in Africa and the West Indies. It is pleasing to know that the irascible theatre manager, who often owed money to his employees, was a political champion of the oppressed at home and abroad.

## 1.2 THE THEATRICAL BACKGROUND

### Theatre Royal, Drury Lane

In order to visualise the way in which *The School for Scandal* was staged in 1777 it is necessary to know a little about the Theatre Royal, Drury Lane. Visitors to the theatre were segregated into three social areas in the auditorium: the boxes, the pit and the galleries. The boxes, which ran along the sides and the rear of the house, accommodated the wealthier of the patrons. On either side of the house a stage box offered its occupants close proximity to the actors. Boxes, along with the rest of the house, were illuminated by candles throughout the performance. At ground level the pit consisted of an area of backless benches ranged on rising steps. Neither space nor comfort could be found here, yet tradespeople, professionals, writers and artists cheerfully crowded into the pit for an evening's entertainment. Above the boxes two galleries carried the remainder of the audience.

The stage of an eighteenth-century theatre was divided into two areas. Nearest to the audience, and thrust into the auditorium, was a flat acting area known as the proscenium. Here actors performed for much of the time. On either side was a proscenium door through which the majority of the entrances and exits were made. The proscenium was backed by a heavily ornate archway; from the rear of this was suspended the theatre's green curtain. When raised, this revealed the second of the stage areas, that on which the scenery was set up. Unlike modern scenery, the settings were painted on a series of wing pieces, slotted along the sides of the stage. These were backed by sliding screens on which more of the setting was depicted. The screens, secured in grooves, could be pulled open by stage-hands, thus allowing the audience to view the next scene. The green proscenium curtain was raised at the start of the play and remained so until the end of the piece. Therefore, the scene changes took place in full view of the audience.

An engraving exists which depicts the scene in Joseph Surface's library. The setting was designed by a Philip James de Loutherbourg (1740-1812), an émigré artist from Alsace. Two wing pieces on either side of the stage consist of heavy Ionic pillars. At the rear of the stage, bookshelves and a window are painted on the shutters. The screen behind which Lady Teazle hides has been placed to the rear of the stage (up-stage), whilst the other characters, Charles, Joseph and Sir Peter, stand on the proscenium.

Lighting was patchy. A row of footlights, oil-burning lamps, ran across the front of the proscenium, lighting the actor, who stood well down-stage. These argand lamps were also used side-stage to illuminate the wing pieces and the shutters. The centre part of the scenes area must often have been a murky place, lit only by a certain amount of over-spill, giving a mottled effect of dark and light patches.

## 1.3  THE THEATRICAL REPERTOIRE

*The School for Scandal* was but one of many entertainments staged in London in 1777. A range of plays was presented in the course of a week, and each evening a main piece and an after-piece were given. Thus a play-going visitor to London could quickly gain an impression of the current repertoire. Sheridan's other comedies, especially *The Duenna* and *The Rivals*, were often performed. One could occasionally see, also, Oliver Goldsmith's (1730-74) golden play *She Stoops to Conquer*. A few of the comedies of William Shakespeare (1564-1616) were popular, although often in a rewritten form; *The Taming of the Shrew*, for example, was recast by David Garrick under the title *Catherine and Petrouchio* and staged as an after-piece.

Most popular, however, were the sentimental comedies of playwrights such as Richard Cumberland (1732-1811) and Hugh Kelly (1739-77). These tended to be moralistic plays in which man was considered as he ought to be, rather than as he lived in the world of reality. Often staged was Cumberland's *The West Indian*, in which we can see the quintessence of the sentimental comedy. It concerns the hero, Belcour, a half-caste, who has come to London from Bermuda. He is an inherently benevolent young man, who responds too generously to the needs of Londoners surrounding him. He is rakish, too, and at one point he goes so far as to attempt to seduce the heroine. Typically of his kind, but improbably, he reforms and then discovers that he is no orphan, as he had imagined, but the son of a prosperous citizen. The heroine, whom eventually he marries, is also, it transpires, blessed with wealth. Throughout the play the dialogue is highly sententious and 'edifying'. The central characters become idealised to an impossible degree; and in the development of the plot their plight and their joys wring pity and gratification from the audience. It is important that these traits are kept in mind in considering Joseph Surface as 'the Man of Sentiment', for he speaks in aphorisms (pithy, moral sayings), and to some, at least, he appears to be a paragon.

Tragedies were popular, too, at this time. Several of Shakespeare's plays in which a self-divided villain held the stage were repeatedly revived, especially *Macbeth* and *Othello*. This figure of the brooding villain appears in many Gothic plays and melodramas of the decade. The settings, within which the villain operates, of ruined castles, subterranean dungeons, wild forests, and storm-rent mountains are significant locations. *Eldred, The Heroine of the Cave* and *Braganza* are but three examples of Gothic dramas.

The London playgoer was offered a rich and varied fare in 1779, and to this Sheridan's briskly moving comedy *The School for Scandal* was a welcome, and subsequently highly popular, addition.

# 2 STUDY METHODS

## 2.1 PRACTICAL STUDY

After he had seen *The School for Scandal*, the Georgian arbiter of taste, Sir Horace Walpole (1717-97), wrote to his friend, the Revd William Mason (1725-97), expressing his delight in the piece. However, the following year, he wrote in another letter to Mason:

> . . .I have *read The School for Scandal*: it is rapid and lively, but is far from containing the wit I expected from seeing it acted.

In these two letters Walpole voices an important point: Richard Brinsley Sheridan's comedy is best appreciated in performance, rather than as a work silently read to oneself. When you have gained some knowledge of the text, see the play on the stage; that is the best way to make the work live in your own experience.

As well as watching the play it is also possible to perform several pages of text as a study method. In order to do this effectively you must visualise clearly the layout of the Georgian stage, which is described in Section 1.2. Let us examine a short scene in the play, and try to reconstruct the way it would have been performed in Sheridan's day. The second scene of the play is set in Sir Peter Teazle's house. Teazle enters through the left proscenium door; in order to speak directly to the audience he may walk down to the footlights; Rowley, the steward, comes from the right proscenium door and joins Teazle for the conversation. No further directions are given until the end of the scene, therefore one has to examine the text carefully for implied stage directions. Rowley's questions and Sir Peter's answers imply that the two men are standing near to each other, perhaps facing, or else partly turned to the audience. However, at the point of their slight disagreement ('You know, Sir Peter, I have always taken the liberty to differ with you. . .'), it would be possible for Rowley to move away from Sir Peter, only to be pursued by him on, 'You are wrong, Master Rowley, you are wrong'. Certainly Rowley's news that Sir Oliver is in London indicates that the two men are standing close together, by that time in earnest conversation. Perhaps Sir Peter's strange circumlocution '. . .he must be soon at my house. . .' (why not simply 'here'?) is a suggestion that Sir Peter has travelled far downstage, near enough to the audience to indicate his house as a separate area upstage. At the end of the scene Sir Peter goes off left, possibly to another room in the house, and Rowley's exit through the proscenium door on the right suggests that he is making his way out into the street.

There are several scenes with which students may care to experiment, for example 2.2, which is set in Lady Sheerwell's home. A prompt book of 1778 states that the only functional furniture in the scene consists of a card table; another copy adds six upright chairs, placed along the back wall. This suggests that many of the characters are left standing, and that those who sit do so formally in a line. The scene poses a number of problems which you may care to solve by experiment. How do you ensure that Sir Benjamin Backbite is in the most important position on stage to read his poem? He is the centre of attention until Mrs Candour attempts to commandeer an audience. How does one arrange the slanderers in order to make the most effective use of their gossip? How do you show, too, that Maria and Sir Peter are not members of this group? Does the joint list of characteristics (Caledonian locks. . .Dutch nose. . .Austrian lip. . .) suggest that Backbite and Crabtree are standing in a visible relationship to each other? How is the incipient affair between Joseph and Lady Teazle demonstrated in their speaking, movements, and eye contact? There are, of course, no set answers to these problems. Students will need to experiment with the text in order to realise its implications.

The complicated screen scene in Joseph's library (4.3) can only be appreciated in performance. Joseph is the person who ties the scene together and it is he who, in drawing people away from both screen and closet determines, by the speed of his movements, the pace of the speaking. It often happens in the theatre that the overall pace of a scene is determined by one or two people. A useful section for practical study is the conversation between Charles and Joseph. Not only is Joseph attempting to keep Charles from both screen and closet, he is also anxious to ensure that Charles is not overheard.

These simple exercises, and there are many more which may be undertaken in studying the play, will help students appreciate not only the relationships which are built up between the various characters as they move on stage, but also the direction, drive and force of the speaking.

## 2.2 TEXTUAL STUDY

A further method of study, one complementary to the practical approach outlined above, is to trace each theme of the plot as it winds its way through the play. The themes consist of the scenes in which the slanderers are featured, the incidents concerning the marriage of the Teazles, the scenes which depict the actions of the two Surface brothers and the encounters between Sir Oliver Surface and his nephews in his own *persona* and those of Mr Premium and Mr Stanley. In tracing these themes, note carefully which characters instigate the action (for example, in the scenes in which the Teazles are portrayed, Lady Teazle is the forceful character who usually sets a train of events in motion), and which characters are preyed upon and deceived. Note carefully, too, what each character does, and what happens to him or her; then compare your list with the analysis of the function of each character which you will find in Section 5.4. In doing this you will begin to understand the way in which this complicated plot is knitted together.

# 3 SUMMARIES AND CRITICAL COMMENTARY

## 3.1 SYNOPSIS

The plot of *The School for Scandal* consists of a number of threads skilfully woven together. The 'school' mentioned in the title consists of the scandalmongers: Mrs Candour, Sir Benjamin Backbite, Crabtree and Snake, who are presided over by Lady Sneerwell. For the duration of the play the young country-born wife of Sir Peter, Lady Teazle, is also an enthusiastic *habituée* of the club. Sir Peter, an elderly gentleman, has only recently become married and he fears for his wife's morals and economic good sense whilst she is finding her feet in London society.

Charles Surface, a good-natured spendthrift, is contrasted with his brother Joseph, a seemingly virtuous man of sentiment, who is, beneath the skin, mean, lusting and self-seeking. Charles is in love with Sir Peter Teazle's niece and ward, Maria, and she returns his love; Joseph is courting her also, but with an eye to her fortune, and at the same time making assignations with Lady Teazle, about which Sir Peter has heard rumours. Sir Oliver Surface, the wealthy uncle of Charles and Joseph, returns unexpectedly from the East Indies. Hearing varying reports of his nephews, he decides to put them to a test of his own devising. He visits Charles, whom he knows to be in financial difficulties, in the guise of a money-lender named Mr Premium. In no time Charles has sold his uncle the family portraits in order to raise money, with the exception of one to which he is attached of an 'ill looking little fellow' (4.1), a likeness of Sir Oliver. The old man develops a fondness for Charles but grows suspicious of Joseph, in spite of frequent plaudits bestowed on him by Sir Peter.

Joseph receives a visit from Lady Teazle and tries to seduce her in his library. Suddenly Sir Peter arrives and Lady Teazle, fearful of being caught in a compromising situation, hides behind a screen. Whilst out of sight, she hears Sir Peter tell Joseph of a settlement he has made on her, although he suspects she is engaged in an intrigue with Charles. Unexpectedly this young man arrives and Joseph is forced to hide Sir Peter in the closet, but not before Sir Peter has discovered that someone ('a little French milliner' (4.3) he is told by Joseph) is secreted behind the screen. A conversation between the two brothers reveals to Sir Peter that his suspicions of Charles are unfounded. On learning that Sir Peter is in hiding, Charles drags him from the cupboard. In Joseph's temporary absence Sir Peter decides to tell Charles of Joseph's affair with the milliner; wishing to peep at her, Charles throws down the screen just as Joseph re-enters the library. Lady Teazle is revealed, as is the hypocrisy of Joseph.

Furthermore, Joseph's meanness is made plain when Sir Oliver visits him, disguised this time as a poor relation, Mr Stanley, applying for financial help. Using the claimed stinginess of his uncle as an excuse, Joseph rejects the plea for help. On the discovery of the true identity of the relative Joseph is totally discredited.

The complicated plot is at the point of resolution. Lady Teazle views her husband in a rosier light and Sir Peter, brushing the discovery of his wife in Joseph's library to one side, determines that they will both live happily together. Charles wins permission from Sir Peter to marry Maria. Lady Teazle takes her leave of the 'scandalous college' (5.3), but not before the repetition of an ill-founded rumour about Sir Peter has made its members appear thoroughly discomforted.


## 3.2 SUMMARIES AND COMMENTARY

### The Prologue

In the eighteenth century prologues were either written by the playwright, or by another person. The prologue for *The School for Scandal* was composed by David Garrick, who wrote many comedies and a quantity of light verse, of which this is representative. Garrick's task is to introduce the subject of the play. It will be noticed that the prologue is arranged in rhyming couplets couched in iambic pentameters. An iambic pentameter is made up of five feet; each foot contains a stressed syllable:

/Last Night/Lord L-/was caught/with La/dy D-/

Thomas King, who played the part of Sir Peter Teazle, spoke this prologue, standing on the proscenium in front of a painted drop curtain.

Wittily, the title of the play is captured in the opening line of the verse: the audience is instantly aware that it is to see a piece about scandalmongers. The speaker gives an imitation of Lady Wormwood (Wormwood is a bitter herb, so she is aptly named) drinking tea and perusing the papers for scandal. Her conversation is an imitation in verse of that of Lady Sneerwell and her companions. The purpose of the playwright, the speaker continues, is a moral one: to attack scandalmongering by exposing it. But is this young author (at the time Sheridan was twenty-six) able to fight successfully a vice as prolific as the many-headed hydra which, when one head is chopped off, grows another? Finally Sheridan's efforts in creating his play (envisaged as a fight) are commended to the audience.

As was usual, Garrick's prologue appeared after the first night in several of the London newspapers, including the *Chronicle* and the *Gazetteer*.

## Act 1, scene 1

*Summary*
The opening scene of the play takes place in Lady Sneerwell's dressing-room in her London house. When the curtain rises Lady Sneerwell and Snake are discovered in conversation: Snake offers his assurances that various snippets of gossip have been inserted in the newspaper. After mentioning Mrs Clackitt as a rumour-monger, attention is focused on Lady Sneerwell who, in her youth, was wounded by 'the envenomed tongue of slander'. Consequently she feels she has a justification for engaging in malicious gossip.

It is Snake who verbally introduces the audience to the brothers Joseph and Charles Surface. Joseph is the elder and Snake describes him as 'possessing the most amiable character', whilst Charles, the younger, is 'the most dissipated and extravagant young fellow in the kingdom'. Maria, the young ward of Sir Peter Teazle, is betrothed to Charles. Joseph Surface, however, seeks Maria's fortune and is anxious to break the match between her and his brother. Lady Sneerwell, for her part, is in love with Charles, and so finds it convenient to aid Joseph in his match-breaking plans. She sees through his virtuous appearance which others admire, and regards him as 'artful, selfish and malicious'. She has discovered a further important trait in him - he is 'a sentimental knave' a term which is discussed in Section 4.3. At this point Joseph Surface arrives: here is an opportunity for Lady Sneerwell to give the audience a further nugget of information: 'I don't wonder at people giving him to me for a lover.' She realises that she herself is the subject of slander.

For a while the talk centres on Charles Surface's growing debts, but this is interupted by the arrival of Maria, who has slipped away from her guardian in order to avoid the unwelcome conversation of Sir Benjamin Backbite, a further member of the slandering community, and himself in love with Maria.

Mrs Candour is announced, and in the moments before she appears the audience learns that she cloaks her gossiping under the disguise of good nature. It is Mrs Candour who brings up the subject of rifts, not only between Maria and Charles, but also between Sir Peter Teazle and his young wife. As the gossip of the town is poured out, we see that Maria is no party to this.

Sir Benjamin Backbite arrives in company with his uncle Mr Crabtree. Momentarily the conversation turns to Backbite's ability to produce rhymed epigrams. The company then discusses the nature of scandal and various scurrilous illustrations are given. Amongst this chatter there is an important (as far as the plot is concerned) snippet of news – Sir Oliver Surface is to return home from the East Indies. Crabtree wonders about Sir Oliver's reactions to the profligacy of his nephew Charles. At the mention of the boy's reckless entertaining, Maria pretends to be unwell and takes her leave. After Maria's departure talk continues about Charles' penury, with Sir Benjamin as the fount of information, until he leaves with his uncle.

A brief coda to the scene consists of Lady Sneerwell inviting Joseph to stay until the late afternoon for dinner.

*Commentary*

In Sheridan's choice of a dressing-room as the location for his opening scene we realise that *The School for Scandal* is a continuation of the tradition of Restoration comedy, in which dressing-room scenes were often employed: an example is to be found in the third act of the comedy by William Congreve (1670–1729), *The Way of the World*. Lady Sneerwell's home is set in the West End of London, a contrast with Sheridan's previous comedy *The Rivals*, in which the setting was the equally fashionable city of Bath. The time of day is not clearly stated, but the audience is left to presume it is during the morning: Lady Sneerwell is attending to her make-up; Maria, on leaving, wishes Lady Sneerwell 'a good morning'; and Snake, according to the stage direction, is drinking chocolate, a morning beverage.

Characters are introduced in the first act of a play. In this scene two groups are brought to the attention of the audience. The first is the company of scandalmongers, headed by Lady Sneerwell herself. Some of these, such as Mrs Candour, Backbite and Crabtree, are introduced on to the stage. Others are simply mentioned in passing, among whom are Lady Brittle and Captain Boastall, Miss Gadabout and Sir Filigree Flirt, and Mrs Fertino and Colonel Castino. It is the nature of scandal to bracket names together as in these instances. The presence of their names helps the audience to feel that the comedy is peopled by a vast throng. By the end of the first scene the audience realises that Sheridan has selected for stricture the dissemination of scandalous gossip and he obviously intends to criticise this by presenting the gossips in a ridiculous light.

Severe
criticism

to scatter
or spread
widely

The second group of characters consists of the Surface brothers, Charles and Joseph, and their uncle, Sir Oliver. Maria must be included in this group, for she is in love with Charles. The plot in which this group is involved is one that has been used on page and stage for many years: the contrast of the wild but essentially good-natured brother with his sibling who appears virtuous, but is streaked with meanness and greed in reality. This contrast between the two brothers is complicated by the overlaid 'sentimentalism' of Joseph Surface. For us today that affectation is difficult to appreciate, but it held a fascination for an eighteenth-century audience.

We notice in this scene one of the marks of Sheridan's dramatic craftsmanship: the stage gradually fills with characters. Before the entry of almost every person a thumbnail sketch is given, so that the audience is in a state of expectation, not only about the person who is to appear, but also his reaction to the pervading group dynamic. Few people leave in the course of the scene and Sheridan makes capital from the departure of Backbite and Crabtree by causing them to return with further information. When repeated, the device is an unfailing way of amusing an audience.

## Act 1, scene 2

*Summary*

From a room in his own house, Sir Peter Teazle speaks directly to the audience: he tells its members that he altered his state from an elderly bachelor to a married man by wedding, six months earlier, a young wife who had been brought up in the country. To his chagrin she has become a fashionable lady of the town, but in spite of this he loves her dearly. Rowley, the steward to the Surface brothers' late father, enters and Sir Peter offloads his vexations on to him. After expatiating on his and Lady Teazle's contrary temperaments (and he believes that the company Lady Teazle keeps with Lady Sneerwell exacerbates the rift), he goes on to complain of Maria's fondness for Charles Surface, whom Sir Peter believes, in common with most other people, to be a ne'er-do-well. He compares him unfavourably with Joseph, whom he dubs 'a Man of Sentiment'; but Rowley attempts to modify Sir Peter's dislike of Charles.

The news we heard in the previous scene is reinforced in this: Sir Oliver Surface has returned to town. Further information is given: Sir Oliver is to test out the moral worth of his two nephews. Sir Peter is more interested in recalling their previous comradeship during his bachelor days; Sir Oliver has remained unwed. Rowley reminds Sir Peter that he and his wife must present at least the appearance of conjugal happiness whilst Sir Oliver visits the couple.

## Commentary

The scene shifts to Sir Peter Teazle's house, which forms a favourable contrast with the gossip-ridden domain in the preceding scene. Sir Peter is engaged, at the beginning, in a convention of the Georgian stage - he addresses the audience directly, laying bare his emotions. It is through Sir Peter and Rowley that we are introduced to the third group of characters in the play - the elderly knight, his young wife and their ward, Maria.

In Sir Oliver Surface's resolution to make a test of the worth of each of his nephews we encounter another strategy of eighteenth-century writers: in the novel by Henry Fielding (1707-54), *Tom Jones*, a seemingly profligate brother is compared with his sententious, but overtly moral, sibling. The writers' sympathies in each case are with the full-blooded, lusty fellow, and at the outset of *The School for Scandal* the audience learns that Joseph is a *poseur* as far as a life of virtue is concerned.

## Act 2, scene 1

### Summary

This scene continues in the same location. The day appears to have progressed to the afternoon. Sir Peter and Lady Teazle are engaged in a ferocious argument; Sir Peter is trying to assert his authority as Lady Teazle's husband; of this, she will have nothing. Sir Peter instances his wife's extravagances - her flowers, her coach and her footmen. Throughout his remonstrances Sir Peter reminds his wife of her own rural origins, and he paints a homely picture of her playing cards (Pope Joan), reading sermons to her aunt, and making music; from these humdrum occupations he has brought her to town to be his wife. Lady Teazle reminds her husband that she has an appointment at Lady Sneerwell's. Sir Peter sums up his opinion of her *habituées* as 'utterers of forged tales, lovers of scandal and clippers of reputation'. However, he agrees to look in briefly in order to guard his reputation. After his wife's exit, Sir Peter muses on the charm with which she enters into arguments with him; if she doesn't appear to love him, a fulfilment is to be found in the quarrelling.

### Commentary

Although the audience has heard much about Sir Peter and Lady Teazle in the first act, this is the first time the couple appear on stage together. Sheridan creates a sparkling and brittle dialogue to accommodate the quarrel. A strong sense of rapid continuity is brought to this by the device of making each character repeat a key word in the terminating phrase of the previous speech. When studying the text it must be remembered that this type of dialogue was accompanied by a lively movement pattern, made the more effectively by the sail of the heavy hooped skirts the

actresses wore. Sir Jonah Barrington (1766-1834), the theatrical historian,
described the effect:

> . . .whenever [the performers] made a speech [they] walked across
> the stage and changed sides with the performer who was to speak
> next, thus veering backwards and forwards, like a shuttlecock. . .

The setting of the first scene reminded the audience of one of the conventions of Restoration comedy. Another is employed in the clear distinction
made between the simplicity of country living and the extravagances and
fashions of the town. Audiences would remember the situation in *The
Country Wife* by William Wycherley (1640-1716) in which Pinchwife had
married a country girl and was fearful that, when transported to London,
she would lose her honour. This Restoration comedy was often played in
Sheridan's days under the title *The Country Girl*, an adaptation by David
Garrick.

### Act 2, scene 2

*Summary*

The scene returns to a room in Lady Sneerwell's house. She and her friends
are admiring an epigrammatic rhyme Backbite has written on the subject
of Lady Curricle's carriage horses. In this he describes them as 'macaronis'.
These were fops, named after members of the Macaroni Club, who wore
very tight-fitting, colourful and exaggerated clothes. Possibly Backbite is
dressed as one of these. Lady Teazle and Maria arrive. Rapidly the conversation becomes a dissection of the manners of absent ladies: the com-
plexions, natural or otherwise, of Miss Vermillion and Mrs Evergreen are
criticised, as well as the mouths and teeth of Miss Simple and Mrs Prim.
Maria is noticeably detached from this conversation.

Sir Peter Teazle arrives, but his presence only momentarily interrupts
the stream of malice. Mrs Pursy's weight is condemned, along with a
description by Lady Teazle of current methods of losing weight: '. . .she
almost lives on acids and small whey'; Miss Sallow's artisan pedigree and
efforts to look younger are criticised; and the face of Mrs Ogle, Mrs
Candour's cousin, is anatomised. Throughout the interchange Sir Peter
makes ineffective pleas that reputations should be preserved, for legal
action can be taken against slanderous remarks, a point which Crabtree
dismisses, believing that there 'never was a slanderous tale without some
foundation'. Sir Peter pretends to be called away by business, wittily
remarking that he is leaving his character behind him.

The majority of the company go upstage for a game of cards, leaving
Joseph and Maria in conversation. Their subject has been broached before
– Maria's neglect of Joseph Surface's attentions in favour of those of Charles.

Kneeling before her, Joseph is surprised by the sudden entry of Lady Teazle. On Maria's departure he attempts to explain his position, claiming that Maria has discovered that Joseph and Lady Teazle have a 'tender concern' for each other and, in consequence, she was threatening to acquaint Sir Peter with the news. Lady Teazle reminds Joseph of his social position – he is no more than the recognised gallant (or *cicisbeo*) of a married townswoman.

Left alone on stage, Joseph Surface recapitulates on his present emotional turmoil: originally he wished to ingratiate himself with Lady Teazle, so that she would not oppose his courtship of Maria but now he himself has become a serious lover of Lady Teazle.

## Commentary

The gossip and chatter in this scene play little part in the advancement of the plot, but they do reflect the exaggerations of the society of the day by concentrating on *minutiae*. However, the plot gains ground in the complications which have beset the affections of Joseph Surface; whilst maintaining the appearance of moral rectitude, he is interested in withdrawing Maria from his brother's affections in order to gain financially, and in developing his courtship of Lady Teazle.

With skill, Sheridan has woven three of the strands of the play together in this scene: the audience has watched Lady Sneerwell's circle at work; Lady Teazle and her husband have entered its orbit; and a statement has been made about Joseph's affections.

## Act 2, scene 3

### Summary

The scene transfers back to Sir Peter Teazle's house. Sir Oliver Surface and Rowley are discussing Sir Peter's marriage. Surface is amused that a confirmed bachelor has wed a young country girl. Rowley reiterates that Teazle is greatly prejudiced against Charles Surface, especially as Sir Peter has heard that Lady Teazle is partial to him. Sir Oliver refuses to be swayed against Charles because of unfounded rumours. Indeed, he sees similarities between himself when young and Charles.

As Sir Peter enters, Surface notes that marriage has altered his appearance; but on a wise prompt from Rowley the conversation quickly changes to Sir Oliver's nephews. Peter Teazle expresses his admiration for Joseph's aphorisms – a point which irritates Oliver. The uncle's final speech in praise of wild youth is an amusing flourish with which to end the scene.

### Commentary

A natural interest is aroused in the audience by the meeting of the two old friends, Peter Teazle and Oliver Surface. Little new information is given to the audience beyond the important fact that Sir Oliver seems to have a natural sympathy with the boisterous nature of Charles, whilst finding Joseph's moralistic view of life an annoyance.

## Act 3, scene 1

*Summary*

With prompting from Sir Peter Teazle and Rowley, Sir Oliver Surface hatches a plan to meet each of his nephews under two separate disguises. He will impersonate Mr Premium, a moneylender, in visiting Charles; and old Mr Stanley, sometime a merchant in Dublin who has fallen on hard times, when he sees Joseph. There are moments of quiet humour as Sir Oliver rehearses his part as a moneylender coached by Moses, an 'honest Israelite', who has already had some financial dealings with Charles Surface. Topical allusions are made to the Annuity Act, passed in the House of Commons shortly before the play's first night, in which minors (people under 21 years of age) were protected from annual payments of interest of more than ten shillings per hundred pounds. Moses accompanies Sir Oliver, giving him further instruction in his newly acquired profession.

When he is alone on stage, Sir Peter ruminates on the reported affair between his wife and Charles Surface; worried, he decides to consult Joseph Surface. On Maria's entry Sir Peter remonstrates with her about her fondness for Charles Surface, whom Sir Peter regards as a profligate young man. He would have Maria look on Joseph with an eye of admiration. Spiritedly, Maria stands up to her guardian.

The last section of the scene is a stage artifice: Sir Peter and Lady Teazle decide that, with as much energy as they have employed in quarrelling, they will vie with each other to see who can be the most obliging – and this in spite of Lady Teazle's demand for two hundred pounds. Rapidly, however, a fresh controversy blows up and Sir Peter threatens to obtain a separation order. The unexpected twist is that Lady Teazle happily agrees to his proposition and her husband is left angry that he fails even to raise his wife to ire.

*Commentary*

The scene is clearly divided into three sections. In the first the characters prepare for a later disguise scene, which has some of the elements of a play-within-a-play, for in assuming a role Sir Oliver is doing more than acting a part: he is able to set up an ironic situation in which he, in complicity with the audience, gains an insight into Charles' true nature. *The Merchant of Venice*, with the central character of Shylock the Jew, was a highly popular play at this time, which possibly accounts for a spate of

Jewish moneylenders in comedies of the period. Sheridan was merely following a current fashion. Obviously, the plot is advanced as Sir Oliver prepares to accost his nephew in the guise of Mr Premium. Similarly Sir Peter, in preparing his plan to speak to Joseph Surface about the alleged intrigue of Charles and Lady Teazle, is also leading the audience further into the complexities of the plot.

The ensuing reconciliation and quarrel of the Teazles is by way of reinforcement rather than of advance. Topics already mentioned are pursued further. We can, today, gain an idea of the dynamism of this section from a brief description left by the mother of Charles Reade (1814-84), the novelist, of Sheridan rehearsing the scene with the first Lady Teazle, Mrs Abington. She had answered Sir Peter's remark, 'No, no, madam, the fault's in your own temper', without sufficient spirit. Sheridan corrected her:

> No, no, that won't do at all. It mustn't be *pettish*. That's shallow - shallow. You must go up stage with, 'You are just what my cousin Sophy said you would be', and then turn and sweep down on him like a volcano. 'You are a great bear to abuse my relations! How *dare* you abuse my relations.'

## Act 3, scene 2

*Summary*
The scene changes to a room in Charles Surface's house. Sir Oliver Surface arrives in the guise of Mr Premium, the moneylender, to visit his nephew. The audience learns that the father of Joseph and Charles left the house to Joseph; it was subsequently bought from him by Charles. Trip, Charles' manservant, announces that his master is occupied with company and that Moses and Premium will have to wait. Sir Oliver uses the time to enquire about life at the house. He discovers that there are three or four footmen who annually earn fifty pounds each, and have to pay for their own outmoded bag-wigs. Charles' habit of borrowing money has filtered down to Trip who enquires of Moses about a loan he is negotiating, for which he will use some of his master's clothes as security.

*Commentary*
The location of this scene is a novelty after the alteration between Lady Sneerwell's house and that of the Teazles. The audience sees the vestibule to the house, probably painted on a drop cloth which would hide preparations for the more elaborate scene following. From the conversation of Sir Oliver with the manservant, Trip, the audience gains an impression of the extravagance in which the household indulges.

## Act 3, scene 3

*Summary*
The scene changes to another room in the house of Charles Surface. Some
prompt books describe it as an 'Antique Hall'. A drinking party is in progress at which Charles presides. Of his guests only Careless and Sir Toby
are named. The talk is mainly in praise of wine, and a censuring of those
who have other priorities. Naturally, conversation shifts to toasts and
Sir Toby proposes a song to responsive womankind.

Trip enters and tells Charles that Moses and Premium have arrived;
Careless wishes the company to have the benefit of meeting them. From
women, the subject of the toast changes to usury, and Premium guardedly
proposes that usury may have 'all the sneers it deserves'. He begins to feel
somewhat uneasy in the company and Careless sweeps the revellers into
the next room for a gambling session.

In reply to Charles' request to borrow money Premium explains that he
would have ro procure this from a friend; consequently he enquires about
Charles' security. The most tangible security he can offer is his relationship
with Sir Oliver and his expectations at Sir Oliver's death. An ironical
exchange ensues in which Sir Oliver, in Premium's person, assures Charles
of his uncle's health and longevity, whilst Charles insists that the East
Indian climate has broken that gentleman. Sir Oliver enquires about other
forms of surety: there is the family plate (all sold!) and a valuable library
(at the auctioneers!!). Charles suggests that the family portraits might act
as a bond, an idea that at first shocks Sir Oliver but one which eventually
he accepts. Careless, who has entered in order to get Charles to join the
revellers, agrees to be the auctioneer in this sale of ancestry.

*Commentary*
An extra dimension is presented by the rowdy, carousing group of young
men, acting as a foil to the domestic scenes at the Teazle's, and those
buzzing with scandal in Lady Sneerwell's house. When Charles proposes a
toast to Maria her surname is enquired of: 'Oh, damn the surname!'
exclaims the young man. Here again, we have a legacy from Restoration
comedy in which young women are without surnames and the married and
widowed lack forenames. The toast song which follows this exchange is
assigned either to Sir Toby or to Careless in various editions of the play: all
hangs on which actor has a mellifluous voice. *The School for Scandal* is a
play which depends heavily on the spoken word and the diversion which
this scene offers is a dramatic necessity.

The conversation between Sir Oliver and his nephew Charles is a highly
polished and entertaining artifice. It offers many opportunities for irony
occasioned by the ignorance of Charles of the true state of affairs,

knowledge which Moses and Sir Oliver share with the audience. An example
of this is the two-line exchange:

> CHARLES   . . .are you acquainted at all with any of my connections?
> SIR OLIVER   Why, to say truth, I am.

Later Charles, again unwittingly, expresses the kernel around which this
scene is developed. Speaking of his uncle's imagined indisposition he
remarks that he is 'so much altered lately that his nearest relations don't
know him'. The phrase may be taken as Charles intends: but the audience
which shares the joke with Sir Oliver can echo his rejoinder: 'That's droll,
egad.'

Sheridan carefully leads up to the auction of the family portraits. He
develops the situation over four scenes: the initial idea of the impersonation; the previous scene in which the dissolute atmosphere first became
apparent; this scene in which the double act of the impersonation and the
auction is conceived, and the next scene in which the mock auction will be
carried out. It should be pointed out that collections of family portraits
were worth a considerable sum of money. At one point in *A Journey to
Bath* by Frances Sheridan (1724–66), the playwright's mother, Sir Jeremy
can 'thank heaven the family pictures are still extant'. Charles would therefore stand to gain richly by their sale. Sheridan reinforces the many
ironical points he has made in the course of the scene with the final
remark of Charles Surface to his uncle: 'When a man wants money, where
the plague should he get assistance if he can't make free with his own
relations?'

### Act 4, scene 1

*Summary*

The characters who leave the stage at the end of the previous scene enter
the portrait gallery in Charles' house. Sir Oliver is still masquerading as
Mr Premium. Charles displays the collection. Careless is given a 'gouty'
chair – perhaps an old one or a chair with a gout stool attached (gout is a
painful swelling of the joint of the big toe, ankle or knee, sometimes caused
by over-drinking port) in which to sit as auctioneer, and, as a mallet, a
roll of the genealogy of the family. Charles' light-hearted quip to Careless,
'. . .you may knock down my ancestors with their own pedigree', receives
an exclamation of disgust from Sir Oliver: he accuses Charles of perpetra-
ting an '*ex post facto* parricide' – that is, he has murdered them after their
deaths.

The auction begins with various portraits sold at ridiculously low prices,
including one by the Restoration court painter, Sir Godfrey Kneller
(1646–1723). However, Charles finds selling the paintings individually a

tedious business and he quickly offers the remaining lot for the sum of three hundred pounds. Sir Oliver fastens on a picture of himself hanging above the settee and asks to purchase it. This affords an opportunity for Careless to make disparaging – and, incidentally, ironic – remarks about the sitter, but Charles resolutely refuses to part with the portrait for, he says, his uncle has been good to him. Instantly, any offence Charles has given by the sale is removed, and Sir Oliver concedes that here is his nephew in spirit as well as by blood: 'A dear extravagant rogue!' he calls him as he takes his leave with Moses.

After his uncle has left, Charles quickly reckons up how much the sale of the pictures has realised: a third of the total sum has to go to Moses in commission fees, leaving Charles 'five hundred and thirty odd pounds'. This happy financial state gives rise to the epigram, 'I find one's ancestors are more valuable relations than I took 'em for!' Rowley enters, but he is allowed to stay only momentarily, for Charles dispatches him with a gift of one hundred pounds to his acquaintance 'old Stanley', Sir Oliver's second impersonation. Lest, however, any think that he is a too rapidly reformed character, Charles springs from the stage determining to play hazard, a game for gamblers.

## Commentary

The principal interest of the auction scene is Sir Oliver Surface in action as Mr Premium the broker. As a foil to the dialogue this scene allows a certain amount of activity as the pictures are sold. It also offers the prospect of a character whom the audience already knows in one role to be viewed in an extended light as a disguise is assumed. Charles' descriptions of the quaint poses of his great-uncle and aunt cause quiet amusement: Sir Richard Raveline (the name is a technical term in fortification), after fighting in the bloodiest of Marlborough's battles at Malplaquet, appears in an old-style wig and regimental uniform; and Sir Richard's sister, Deborah, assumes the affected pose of a shepherdess feeding her flock. There is a sentence in *The Vicar of Wakefield* by Oliver Goldsmith which suggests the artificiality of this portrait: 'Sophia was to be a shepherdess, with as many sheep as the painter could put in for nothing.' Charles points out one portrait of a sometime Mayor of Manchester, and eighteenth-century actors' texts suggest that the name of the town was altered in order to amuse provincial audiences – thus introducing a note of topicality.

It seems unlikely that on so thin an issue as the refusal to sell a portrait of his uncle, Charles should edge his way permanently into his uncle's affections, but comedy hangs on these conventions which beg credibility. The notion is as easily accepted as that the convention of disguise is impenetrable by those on whom the deceit is practised. For the sake of the plot, an eighteenth-century audience happily accepted these unlikely but popular and long-standing conventions.

## Act 4, scene 2

### Summary
The setting is the parlour in the house of Charles Surface. It may be the same room in which 3.2 was set. None of the faults relating to Charles Surface, which Moses itemises, disturb Sir Oliver: he happily repeats his refrain, '. . .he wouldn't sell my picture'. His regard for his nephew increases when Rowley presents him with the one hundred pounds which had been despatched to 'Stanley'. In this *persona* Sir Oliver is ready to go and meet Joseph Surface. However, Rowley cautions that there must be a delay: Sir Peter is visiting Joseph at the moment.

### Commentary
This scene is an opportunity to wind down after the amusement of the previous one. It is an opportunity for Sheridan to reinforce the satisfaction Sir Oliver Surface feels with his nephew. The next stage of the plot, the visit to Joseph Surface, again a visit of a testing nature, is introduced. In order that the playwright may draw back into the play the theme of the relationship between Joseph and Lady Teazle, which has been left pending during the preparations for, and fruition of, the auction scene, Rowley makes Sir Oliver delay the visit.

## Act 4, scene 3

### Summary
From the house of Charles Surface the scene is transferred to that of his brother Joseph. The setting is the library. A screen, an important piece of furniture in this scene, stands at the rear of the stage.

A servant enters and informs Joseph that Lady Teazle is arriving, having taken the precaution of leaving her sedan chair at the bonnet-makers in a nearby street. Joseph asks the servant to draw the screen across the window in case Lady Teazle should be seen from the opposite houses.

Lady Teazle enters on her clandestine visit and immediately pours out her troubles to Joseph: Sir Peter is ill-tempered and jealous of Charles, whom he fears is fond of Lady Teazle, and Lady Sneerwell is spreading slanderous tales about her. Joseph advises that she should forget her own reputation and enter into a 'trifling *faux-pas*'; this would silence her detractors, for it was really her innocence which gave rise to conjecture and gossip.

Joseph is interrupted in his discourse by the news that Sir Peter Teazle has arrived. Lady Teazle is distraught, and hides herself behind the screen, whilst Joseph pretends to read.

Sir Peter enters and admires the library and the screen ornamented with maps, ironically describing it as a 'source of knowledge'. The purpose of Sir Peter's visit is to unburden himself to Joseph: he fears that his wife is in love with Charles Surface. What is worse, if the liaison were to be discovered, Sir Peter would, as the elderly cuckolded husband, be made the laughing-stock of the town. Joseph affects a mock horror of his brother's supposed adultery. Sir Peter goes on to tell Joseph of the financial settlement he plans to make on his wife: whilst he lives she will enjoy an independent income of eight hundred pounds a year, and after his death the bulk of his estate will pass to her.

Sir Peter proposes to discuss Joseph's courtship of Maria, but Joseph, terrified that Lady Teazle will hear of this from behind the screen, begs Sir Peter not to broach the subject. Joseph is rescued from this predicament by news of the arrival of Charles. Sir Peter wishes to conceal himself so that he may hear Joseph confront Charles about his love for Lady Teazle. He lights on the screen as a hiding place, only to notice a petticoat protruding from it. Affecting a gay laugh, Joseph pretends that he has hidden there 'a little French milliner' who is accustomed to plague him. Quickly he bundles Sir Peter into a closet or cupboard-room. The humour of the situation is increased as Lady Teazle and her husband both peep from behind their places of concealment, yet each remains hidden from the other.

Charles enters from the street, slightly puzzled that Sir Peter has left so soon, to be taxed by Joseph immediately about his attempts to gain Lady Teazle's affections, an accusation which amuses Charles inordinately. He confesses that he has always imagined that Joseph was Lady Teazle's favourite, and starts to enlarge on Joseph's entanglements. He is stopped from further reminiscence as Joseph in a whisper explains that Sir Peter is hiding in the closet. Instantly Charles drags the elderly husband from his hiding place, and intimates that he has some news for him.

A servant announces that a caller waits below. Joseph is in a dilemma, for he must separate Sir Peter and Charles. In leaving, he manages to warn Teazle not to mention the 'French milliner'. Charles enlarges on his brother's moral position as a Man of Sentiment to such an extent that Sir Peter, unable to contain the secret any longer, tells him of the prize behind the screen. Charles rushes up-stage and topples the screen just as Joseph returns. Sir Peter is horrified to see that his wife is the 'milliner'. Charles' parting remark condemns his brother's lack of probity.

The remaining company stand in silence looking at each other. Lamely, Joseph makes his explanation: Lady Teazle had realised Joseph's feelings for Maria, and has called in order that he might explain his position; on Sir Peter's arrival she was fearful of her husband's jealousy and hid behind the screen. Lady Teazle denies there is any truth in Joseph's story; she came to the house because, she says, she was seduced by 'insidious arguments', and wished to listen to Joseph's 'pretended passion'. In a speech of considerable dignity she acknowledges that Sir Peter's expressions of tenderness have reformed her affections, and that her future life will be a sincere expression of gratitude. As Sir Peter and his wife leave the library, Joseph follows, offering lame protestations.

## Commentary

The skilful construction of the scene, and Sheridan's deft use of situation, make it not only the climax of *The School for Scandal*, but also one of the highlights of the eighteenth-century stage. From the scenes in the houses of Lady Sneerwell, the Teazles and Charles Surface, the audience is now taken into the library of Joseph Surface. Here, several of the threads of the plot are drawn together: these are Joseph's intrigue with Lady Teazle, Joseph's courtship of Maria, the relationship between Sir Peter Teazle and his wife, and the different natures of the two brothers, Charles and Joseph. The ploy of placing one or two *voyeurs* behind a screen was used in eighteenth-century drama: Goldsmith, for example, so conceals Hardcastle and Sir Charles Marlow that they may learn about Marlow's relations with Kate in *She Stoops to Conquer*; but the device of hiding two people, each at a separate point of seclusion, offers fresh dramatic possibilities to the playwright. In the former case the people hidden are advantaged by their gains in knowledge; in this particular scene the balance of the power of knowledge is transferred from one to another as details which one secluded person would not wish the other hidden partner to hear threaten to become public. This device of the double seclusion also increases the pace of the scene as its 'regulator', in this case Joseph, has continually to take cognizance of the possible implications of the information passing from one party to another.

In the sudden fall of the screen and the revelation of Lady Teazle a climax is reached, not limited to the Teazles' thread of the plot, but for the play as a whole. The disintegrative effects of scandal are made plain. Sheridan would seem to have regarded this as the climactic moment, for in his direction of the piece the characters on stage held a highly dramatic pause after the fall of the screen; so long, in fact, that David Garrick wrote to Sheridan suggesting that this pause was 'carry'd to too great a length'.

With the audience aware that neither of the hidden people knows of the presence of the other, and the added fact that people passing through know only of the existence of one of the pair, the situation is replete with ironical implications which Sheridan uses to the full. There is the 'private business' of Sir Peter which he unfolds in his wife's hearing, spiked with the repeated use of the term 'discovery'; Joseph's denouncement of his brother's supposed cuckoldry of Sir Peter furthers an opportunity to engage irony in a moral purpose; Sir Peter insists that his wife is not to know of his settlement on her, as unbeknown she listens to him; and Sir Peter's hapless attempts to get Joseph to trap his brother Charles into an admission of Charles' affections for Lady Teazle. The screen and the closet have become visible symbols of the semi-secrecy of the whispered gossip of Lady Sneerwell's circle which, as here, ultimately reaches its subjects.

## Act 5, scene 1

*Summary*
The scene continues in the library in Joseph's house. There would appear to be a slight time lapse between this and the preceding scene.

To Joseph's annoyance his servant has let in Sir Oliver Surface in his second disguise, that of Mr Stanley, the poor relation. Joseph summarises for the audience the disasters which struck him: 'My character with Sir Peter, my hopes with Maria, destroyed in a moment.' He then leaves the stage.

When Sir Oliver and Rowley enter, they are surprised that Joseph is not waiting to receive them. His absence affords opportunity for the pair to make their unfavourable estimate of the young man. Rowley decides that he will go and, once the interview has ended, he will return and acquaint Joseph that Sir Oliver, in his own *persona*, has arrived. Before 'Mr Stanley' can plead his case, Joseph has hastily assured him that Sir Oliver, although a worthy man, has been of no financial help to him, giving him only an occasional present. In his aside to the audience Sir Oliver informs the house that he has given Joseph twelve thousand pounds. Joseph goes on to blame his brother Charles, to whom he says he has lent much, for his present depleted finances. Before the formal pleasantries of departure, Joseph cloaks his unwillingness to help Stanley in a sententious remark: 'To pity without the power to relieve is still more painful than to ask and be denied.'

Sir Oliver's departure was the prearranged cue, promptly taken up, for Rowley's re-entry. He hands Joseph a note that Sir Oliver Surface has arrived in town and that he and Charles will be visiting him shortly. Joseph's principal concern is to find Stanley, lest he should report his disadvantageous interview to Sir Oliver.

*Commentary*
This disguise scene lacks the high spirits of the earlier incident of the sale of the family portraits to Mr Premium. After the activity of the previous scene a short interlude in a quieter key is necessary. Nevertheless, the sight of Sir Oliver in a series of disguises does provide additional interest, and the selfishness of Joseph is admirably exemplified in this brief incident.

## Act 5, scene 2

*Summary*
The scene reverts to Sir Peter Teazle's house. Mrs Candour has called in order to attempt to learn at first hand about the incident with the screen. Sir Benjamin Backbite arrives, presumably on the same mission. Mrs Candour's version of the episode has already become distorted, for she thinks Lady Teazle has been discovered with Charles Surface, although Backbite attempts to correct her. Lady Sneerwell enters and the conversation veers towards the fiction of a duel with swords or, as Crabtree claims on his entry, with pistols. Crabtree has composed an elaborate story about a chest wound which Sir Peter has sustained. Lady Sneerwell leaves, alarmed, in order to glean further information. When Sir Oliver enters he is mistaken for the doctor and plied with questions about the patient's injuries.

The presence of Sir Peter is the only way to stop and disprove the flood of rumours. However, the curiosity and taunts of the town are worse to him than physical wounds and in a threefold command to leave the house he drives out Candour, Backbite and Crabtree. Rowley and Sir Oliver inform Sir Peter, with some amusement, that they too have heard about the 'little French milliner'. Naturally, Sir Peter is discomforted, especially when their mirth begins to turn to hilarity. Sir Oliver leaves in order to return (as himself) to Joseph's house and Rowley explains that he has arrived to plead with Sir Peter as a mediator on Lady Teazle's behalf. Through the door the two men can see her. She is tearfully repentant, but even so, endearingly elegant in Sir Peter's estimation. The men leave the stage, Sir Peter to become reconciled with his wife and Rowley to return to Joseph Surface's house.

*Commentary*
The rapidity of gossip and scandal is made clear in the early part of the scene. For the first time in the play the group of scandalmongers enters Sir Peter's house. He demonstrates in his person that the rumours are totally unfounded. The audience senses that there is little more to be explored in this thread of Sheridan's comedy.

The story of the adjustment of the young country bride to her elderly urban husband seems to be drawing to a satisfactory conclusion as well. Extravagant and flighty as Lady Teazle has been, and as pompous as her husband has been, an intrinsic moral worth shines through the two characters, and the scene ends on an optimistic note.

## Act 5, scene 3

*Summary*
The setting is the library in the house of Joseph Surface. Lady Sneerwell is furious that she has joined in league with 'such a blunderer' as Joseph. She claims that Joseph possesses 'an avarice of crimes': he has imposed upon Sir Peter and attempted to seduce his wife. Snake, Joseph tells Lady Sneerwell, has undertaken to prove that Charles Surface has vowed that Lady Sneerwell shall be his wife; letters in Snake's possession will serve as evidence. Supposing that a knocking at the door heralds the arrival of Sir Oliver, Lady Sneerwell retires.

Joseph is mortified to find the caller is not, as he imagines, his uncle, but instead, Mr Stanley, who refuses to leave as Joseph wishes. Joseph starts to bundle out Sir Oliver when he is met by Charles Surface, who recognises Sir Oliver as Mr Premium. Both brothers wish, before Sir Oliver materialises, to eject the caller, whether he be Stanley or Premium, so they begin forcefully to escort him to the door. The device of an interrupted exit is repeated as the Teazles, Maria and Rowley enter.

Sir Oliver's true identity is immediately established when Sir Peter greets his old friend. The two elderly men and Lady Teazle denounce the meanness and treachery of Joseph. Charles, fearing that he will fare even more harshly, is pleasantly surprised to find that he has won a place in Sir Oliver's affections. Lady Teazle points out that Charles is anxious to gain his uncle's approval for his intended marriage to Maria. Modestly, however, Maria, who has heard of the reported affair between Charles and Lady Sneerwell, offers to relinquish any claim to him.

Lady Sneerwell unexpectedly emerges from the closet where she has been hiding and accuses Charles of unfaithfulness to her. Snake arrives, presumably to support her in her claim; however, Rowley points out that Snake comes in order to confront Lady Sneerwell: the correspondence, the so-called evidence, is forged. At this juncture Lady Teazle dissociates herself totally from Lady Sneerwell's circle. Furious, the latter leaves, maliciously hoping that Sir Peter will give Lady Teazle fifty years of marriage.

Snake takes his leave of the company, begging that the moral stance he has taken will not be noised abroad, for his reputation may suffer. He sums up his position in an epigram: 'I have nothing but my infamy to depend on. . .'.

Now the impediments that rumour had planted are removed, Sir Oliver proposes that the marriage of Charles and Maria should take place the next day and Sir Peter's toast to the couple adds warmth to the ending of the play: '. . .may you live as happily as Lady Teazle and I intend to do!'

*Commentary*
The final scene of a play is a time for the revelation of the truth and for loose ends to be drawn together. Sir Oliver Surface, having put each of his nephews to the test, is recognised in his own person; Lady Sneerwell's plot to discredit Charles is brought to light by means of Snake's uncharacteristic truthfulness; and Joseph's hypocrisy is further unveiled. Moral propriety wins the day: Lady Teazle's dissociation from the scandalmongers is an indication of their worthlessness. In contrast, there is positive joy in the prospect of married bliss, both that of the two young lovers, Maria and Charles, and that of the Teazles now that they have come to terms with each other. This hope for the future is reflected in the stage picture at the end of the play: in Joseph's library, the place where deceit was unveiled by Charles, the two couples stand facing the future, presided over by Sir Oliver, who has been responsible for much of the truth coming to light, together with Rowley, the revered and honest retainer.

Rhymed couplets round off the scene. They may have been added after the play's first season.

**Epilogue**
The epilogue was spoken in character by Mrs Abington (Lady Teazle); it was the usual practice for the leading lady to do this. George Colman the Elder (1732-94), a lively playwright and manager of the Haymarket Theatre, wrote this epilogue. Its main purport is that Lady Teazle has learned the foolishness of dedicating her life to the fashions of London, and therefore she must return to the quiet of the country. Humour lies in the fact that the town life still holds fascination for her and the irony is pointed by Colman's parody (lines 32-42) of a passage from *Othello* (3.3.349 ff.): a farewell to soldiering. Colman used many of his plays as moral vehicles and, light-hearted as his epilogue is, he painstakingly weaves a moral into the last four lines.

# 4 THEMES AND ISSUES

## 4.1 A SATIRE ON SLANDER

In *The School for Scandal* Sheridan presents his audience with a picture of gossips and scandalmongers. This company and its brittle repartee can be used to amuse: hence *The School for Scandal* is a comedy. It is, however, more than this, for Sheridan does not simply record, he also states his own response. In the portraits he draws of Backbite, Crabtree, Sneerwell and Candour it is evident he is ridiculing the participants of the monstrous academy he has set up, and so the playwright creates a satire. It would be possible to condemn the vice of slander in a direct fashion, but this would make Sheridan a moralist, and in his portrayal of Joseph Surface, Sheridan draws attention to the pitfalls awaiting the moralist. Satire is more deadly that direct condemnation, for it draws to its aid biting wit and it places the subjects of its attack in a dreadful position, that of ridicule. Men can stand criticism or condemnation; but ridicule, the undermining of human dignity, is almost impossible to bear.

Why Sheridan chose this particular vice to attack is difficult to decide. He was not notably enmeshed in a web of intrigue and gossip in 1777. Slander was not prevalent to a greater degree in London in that decade than in earlier days. Surely, a stronger impetus to create a satire is needed than the occasional Tête-à-Tête paragraphs which appeared in the *Town and Country Magazine*? Sufficient that Sheridan did decide to highlight this undesirable aspect of human intercourse and in order to strengthen his attack he aligned slander with the vice of hypocrisy: the first is a case of detraction, the second the assumption of the appearance of virtues which one does not in reality possess. Numbers of the characters scrabble for virtue as if its acquisition is a commercial gain: Joseph is the obvious example, but Mrs Candour too possesses 'a very gross affectation of good nature and benevolence' (1.1); we can even see a parallel of this in Backbite's display of rhyming epigrams, for the production of these does not, in any way, turn him into a poet. Many people, Sheridan says within the framework of the play, are not what they seem.

But Sheridan is an optimist. Human nature, although fallible, is essentially virtuous, and we recognise almost immediately those characters who reflect benevolence. In spite of his tantrums, Sir Peter Teazle obviously does so; in spite of his buckishness, Charles Surface does so; in spite of his need for regard, Sir Oliver Surface does so. In these people the essential goodness of humanity shines through their foibles. It is these qualities of warmth and hope which distinguish Sheridan's outlook from that of the earlier Restoration satirists. For playwrights such as William Wycherley humankind was more self-interested and possessive than Sheridan portrayed it.

## 4.2 THE COMEDY OF MANNERS

Nevertheless, we may view *The School for Scandal* as the last of a line of comedies stemming from the Restoration playwrights' view of society and manners. Many of these present the society of the town as the only true society: one comes up, or in the case of the newly-wedded Margery Pinchwife in *The Country Wife* is brought up, to town in order to fit into a complicated social jigsaw. Rural England is at the world's end. It is to London (or in its hey-dey, to Bath) that one must travel in order to participate in society. The coinage of this society is wit, rather than money. Wit will gain most commodities, and people, titles and honours are considered goods for the grasping. Thus an epigrammatic form of language is the norm in post-Restoration comedies, as much in *The School for Scandal* as in earlier works. All the characters join in the parry and thrust of argument and the creation of scintillating philosophies with a facility that is improbable, yet is accepted as the vehicle of conversation in these comedies. Allied to this is the playwrights' habit of highlighting on stage the artifices of urban society within the terms of the dramatic conventions of the day. The very gathering together of the slanderers in *The School for Scandal* is an accepted artifice; it is a convention of the stage to exclude the virtuous from this kind of company, and so Maria eschews it and Lady Teazle renounces it. We are confronted with the conventional difficulties of the elderly married man and his young wife; such pairs of characters can be regarded as part of the stock of the dramatic tradition. The contrast of virtue with vice within the same family is another convention of the dramas, as well as the novels, of Sheridan's day. This highlighting of the artifice of society's conventions, combined with the utilisation of witty dialogue, were important constituents of the 'comedy of manners'. The dramatic critic William Hazlitt (1778-1830), on the place Sheridan held

within this *genre*, remarked that he had 'brought the comedy of n
to the highest perfection, and *The School for Scandal* remains to this
the most popular comedy in the English language'.


## 4.3 'SENTIMENT' AND 'SENTIMENTAL'

Early in the play reference is made to Joseph Surface as both a 'Sentimental Knave' and as a 'Man of Sentiment'. The words 'sentiment' and 'sentimental' which came into recorded use around 1740, held two connotations in the eighteenth-century and both are employed in references to Joseph Surface. The first connotation is of a thought expressed in words. This usually arises from a particular circumstance (for example, Sir Oliver, in the guise of Mr Stanley, asking Joseph for financial help) and leads on to a generalised maxim ('. . .avarice, Mr Stanley, is the vice of age' (5.1)). It is plain to see that these maxims can easily become so generalised that they are but empty bombast; in Sheridan's hands they not only become so, but their hollowness admirably reflects characteristics of Joseph himself. It was late in the writing of the play that Sheridan realised the comic possibilities which could arise by clothing Joseph with sententious aphorisms. These Joseph stores as if they were a form of currency, to be spent at the right moment: 'I'll keep that sentiment till I see Sir Peter' (1.1).

The second meaning which the word holds is an elaborate concept. F. W. Bateson neatly summarised it as the 'primary English shorthand for the *enjoyment* of private emotion for its own sake'. An example may clarify. An emotion which cultured eighteenth-century folk enjoyed was melancholy. It was held to be an emotion which cleansed the feelings in preparation for new sensations. This emotion could be intensified by giving the recipient the optimum physical conditions for its enjoyment. Many an eighteenth-century garden, Stourhead in Wiltshire is an example, contained a small grotto through which water flowed, creating a dark and dank cave. A stone seat would be placed in the grotto and here the sentimentalist could sit and consider those images which would flood him with melancholy. A man of sentiment is a cultured person who can open his heart and mind to private emotions and savour these in quiet contemplation. Through this practice his emotions become refined. Many an eighteenth-century gentleman 'collected' emotional experiences which he could later recall in private. This is that 'emotion recollected in tranquillity' of which William Wordsworth (1770–1850), the Lakeland poet, wrote.

Joseph Surface is too much of an activist to be truly the man of sentiment in this meaning of the word. He is a person unfitted for that solitude which is a requisite for savouring at length private emotions: on first sighting him he is surrounded by the slanderers; the babble of their noise is ntemplation. Later in the play, when he is interrupted pretence of reading, the reality of which is a highly lulging in the recollection of emotions, he quickly y. Palmer, when playing the character, stressed im- the book to the far end of the room. Although accoutrements of the man of sentiment, his library, ment or finer feelings, his emotional reactions, these are merely appearances. The reality is that Joseph is grasping, self-centred, and emotionally sealed from the needs of other people.

## 4.4 CONCEALMENT AND DISGUISE

A further theme which the play explores is the use of concealment. Some-times characters conceal their true *persona* behind a disguise; the two charades which Oliver Surface plays in the guise of Mr Premium and Mr Stanley are examples of this. Other characters adopt lesser, temporary disguises. For a short period of time Sir Peter Teazle pretends to live in a state of contented matrimony for fear that his friend Sir Oliver will tease him. For a longer time Lady Teazle pretends she has a natural affinity with the slanderers and can fit into their company with ease; the vehemence with which she rejects the group reveals that this is only a self-delusion. When disguises are adopted these allow the practitioner to become a de-tached observer of life on which he comments, sometimes to others on stage and sometimes directly to the audience.

Concealment, too, occurs when people go into hiding, as Lady Teazle does behind the screen and Sir Peter does in the cupboard. Here again they are secluded observers of life, for Sheridan makes sure that each is in a position to be aware of what is happening on stage. Whether concealed by disguise or by hiding, the situation is redolent with irony: this the play-wright exploits as a source of humour, at times of black humour. In Section 5.3 comment is made on Sheridan's use of irony.

## 4.5 A PORTRAIT OF THE TOWN

### Scandal in word and in print

The last theme to be extrapolated from the play text is one of which Sheridan was probably not aware at the time of writing *The School for Scandal*. He presents the audience with a picture of urban society in his day. To Sheridan this factual rooting of the play in the present was a way of making it immediate and alive. To present readers, however, tackling the text two hundred years later, Sheridan is acting as the social historian of his day. Primarily, Sheridan portrays the part he feels gossip and scandal play in the life of those who dwell in the fashionable areas of London. In satirising this he leaves the audience to draw its own conclusion that the spread of slander is a destructive vice: this spectators can do as soon as rumour usurps fact in the reports of Sir Peter's reaction on discovering his wife in Joseph's library.

The realisation that wit and conversation require a productive outlet led to the foundation of a number of intellectual salons. One of these was the salon set up in the house of Mrs Elizabeth Montagu which became known as the Blue Stocking circle. Members would hold conversations on literary topics in which eminent men of letters often took part also. Mrs Hannah More (1745-1833), in her poem 'Bas Bleu' wrote:

> At length the mental shades decline,
> Colloquial wit begins to shine;
> Genius prevails and conversation
> Emerges into *reformation*.

Would Lady Sneerwell and Mrs Candour, placed in a different circle, have been capable of such reformation?

Sheridan comments too on the use to which newspapers were put. Snake uses the papers as an extension of verbal slander. Direct reference is made to the scandalous Tête-à-Tête which appeared in issues of the *Town and Country Magazine*. This may be viewed as a real example, although a somewhat mild one, of the mischief a man such as Snake could cause.

Worthless literary endeavours are further exemplified in the verses of Sir Benjamin Backbite. Unlike the authors of the Tête-à-Tête, Backbite believes it is 'very vulgar to print' (1.1) and most of his epigrammatic poems are disseminated verbally. Backbite's poetry reflects his own image, for he himself has the characteristics of a 'macaroni', which he uses as a metaphor in his verse. The slanderers all affect an interest in Backbite's rhymes, but it is the gossiping subject matter rather than an interest in poetry which is the attracting magnet.

## Picture galleries and libraries

Private libraries and picture galleries are also featured in the play, but, as with verse-writing, these hardly denote an interest in literature or painting. Both rooms appear to be those of a cultivated man; but both rooms in the play belie the reality. Joseph is bereft of intellectual curiosity and Charles is only too anxious to sell the portraits in his gallery. Nevertheless, Sheridan realises that they are the accoutrements of civilised households and accordingly uses them as settings in his play. Collecting on a prodigious scale was one of the characteristics of the eighteenth century. Paintings, especially those of the highly popular European landscape artists, Claude Lorraine

(1600-82), Nicolas Poussin (1594-1665) and Salvador Rosa (1615-73) were acquired on the journey by landed gentry making the Grand Tour across the Continent, over the Alps and down to the toe of Italy. Portraiture, too, was popular, and many a family was painted sitting in a park or in an elegant and sparsely furnished room at home by such artists as Arthur Devis (1711-87) and John Wootton (1682-1764). The provision of a picture gallery to house these works helped to establish the reputation of the cultured collector.

The assembling of libraries was equally a sign of cultivated taste. In this period the great collections of such men as Edmund Malone (1741-1812), the literary critic, and Horace Walpole, the Gothic enthusiast and letterwriter, were gathered. The popularity of circulating libraries (of which by the end of the century there were 122 in London) demonstrates, too, that reading was a popular and expanding pastime.

### Sheridan as social historian
Thus it is that Sheridan, in establishing a verisimilitude for his setting, brings to the modern audience a fascinating, first-hand introduction to the London society of his day and to its modes of operating. A play is not written with the ascribed purpose of serving as primary source material for a study of the period: on the other hand, many a play, and Sheridan's is one, serves this purpose admirably.

# 5 TECHNICAL FEATURES

## 5.1 STRUCTURE OF THE PLAY

**The two themes**

In 1825 one of Sheridan's biographers, Thomas Moore (1779-1852) referred to two manuscripts titled 'Sir Peter Teazle' and 'The Slanderers': he suggested that these were two separate plays and that *The School for Scandal* was formed by their fusion. He went on to claim that the flaws he perceived in the plot and characterisation of Sheridan's comedy were due to this conflation. The amalgam of the two plots, he said, gave the comedy 'that excessive opulence of wit, with which, as some critics think, the dialogue is overloaded'. However, the most recent editor of Richard Brinsley Sheridan's works, Professor Cecil Price, has expressed doubts that 'The Slanderers' and 'Sir Peter Teazle' were intended by the author to be separate plays; instead, he views the two sets of manuscripts as drafts for parts of a unified work. Whichever view is adopted, the manuscripts enable us to see that from his initial thoughts about the play Sheridan certainly developed two themes. One is concerned with the domestic life of the Teazles, a familiar enough eithteenth-century plot. The other revolves around a body of gossips engaged in malicious slander. A further motif was later developed: the comparison of the two brothers Surface, including the moral trial which their uncle, Sir Oliver, makes of them.

**The slanderers**

The audience views the slanderers in different lights. In the first scene of the play they are employed by Sheridan on two counts. The first is to give an atmosphere of tittle-tattle and fashionableness. In this role the audience accepts the characters at their face value, giving little credence to the content of the gossip. However, Sheridan also uses this group of people to introduce many characters in the play to the audience, and in order for this dramatic device to work a certain trust must be placed in the information which the gossips convey. Today, amusement is the principal reaction to the gossips' chatter at the beginning of the play. For some eighteenth-century members of the audience the reaction was one of impatience: 'I wish these people would have done talking,' remarked a friend of Thomas Moore during the second act, 'and let the play begin'. To some extent this is a just reaction, for the slanderers do not engage in the mechanics of the plot. They only offer waspish comment as other people, the Teazles and the Surfaces, live their lives.

Amusement turns to condemnation when the audience views the slanderers making capital out of the plight of Sir Peter Teazle, with whom the spectators identify when he is discomforted at his wife's discovery in Joseph's library. Sir Peter driving the gossips from his house is a symbol of the victory of satire over the vice it is attacking. Thus the scenes in which the slanderers appear at the beginning and near the end of the play form a framework to the rest of the comedy; and it is in the intervening sections that situation and activity occur.

### The Teazles and the Surfaces

The theme of the Teazles' marriage and the themes of the comparison and testing of the two brothers have their points of interaction. The audience hears of the affection of Charles for Sir Peter's ward Maria, although it is not until near the conclusion of the play that the two lovers are permitted to appear together. It was as if, remarked Thomas Moore, Sheridan could not trust the two performers with a romantic scene. Joseph's fondness for Maria ('or her fortune' (1.1) remarks Lady Sneerwell) is expressed by Lady Sneerwell early in the play, and by the second act the audience sees Joseph wooing Maria: 'Is hope to be denied the tenderest passion?' (2.2). Immediately afterwards, Joseph's conversation with Lady Teazle prompts from her the remark: 'You are an insinuating wretch!'

It is in the screen scene in the fourth act that the two strands of the plot, those dealing with the Surfaces and the Teazles, are woven together as Joseph hides Lady Teazle behind the screen, only to be revealed by Charles. This is the scene which, Moore states, was recast more than any other in the play, and certainly the unveiling of Joseph's secrets by various characters caught in the maze-trap of the library is an example of masterly dramatic construction. As it stands the scene is a great advance on Sheridan's original idea of effecting a discovery through the mistake of muddled identity. Moore gives the gist:

> Making love to aunt and niece – meeting wrong in the dark – someone coming – locks up the aunt – thinks it to be the niece.

Today we tend to accept and applaud the artifice of the wife hidden behind the screen and her husband in the closet. However, the eighteenth-century audience was harassed by the contrivance. The remark in the *Morning Chronicle* (24 May 1777) is typical:

> The grand situation in the fourth act, is founded in improbability, and though managed with a degree of art, which shows superior judgement, asks for great allowance from the spectator.

There was a feeling, too, that the discovery had taken place too early in the play; enough had been revealed about the character of Joseph. Further revelations merely made the final act 'heavy and tiresome' wrote the critic of the *St James' Chronicle* (13-15 May 1777). Not even the reappearance of the slanderers with their palpably incorrect 'news' could, it was felt, redeem the *longeurs* of the remaining scenes.

## Sir Oliver Surface's disguises

Sir Oliver's testing of his two nephews is an important development in the theme concerning the Surfaces. In each test Sir Oliver disguises himself; when approaching Charles he becomes Mr Premium, the broker, and on meeting Joseph he assumes the guise of Mr Stanley, the poor relation. The disguise has the effect of turning each of these two scenes, especially the auction of the portraits, into an interlude as Sir Oliver acts his fiction. It would be beyond the accepted bounds of the drama for Sir Oliver to alter his nature totally; but within the convention of the disguise he is able to play another character and so draw the interest of the audience in watching his reactions to situations which are often redolent with irony. Some would see a parallel between Sir Oliver concealing himself behind a disguise, and the Teazles closeting themselves behind screen and cupboard door. In this hidden situation each learns opinions about himself which in other circumstances would be difficult.

The disguise as Mr Premium offers Sheridan more opportunities to develop the situation than does the Stanley episode. No draft of the auction scene has been found, and it must be supposed that it was conceived later. Cecil Price has drawn attention to the advertisement for a puppet show in the *Morning Chronicle* (23-28 December 1775) from which the author may have gleaned the germ of an idea:

THE AUCTION ROOM;
A MORNING SCENE
Where will be exhibited and described a Number
of PAINTINGS
Particularly, several ALLEGORICAL FIGURES.

Arthur Murphy, the playwright, complained (wrongly, we would probably judge today) that the auction scene seemed flat with Oliver Surface as the sole bidder, and he suggested that the slanderers should make the event a public occasion, a suggestion which Sheridan ignored. Possibly he wished the attention of the audience to be focused solely on the reaction of each of the Surface brothers to the fictional character by whom he was confronted. There are less theatrical fireworks in the meeting of Joseph and Mr Stanley than in the meeting of Charles with Mr Premium. Already, in the screen scene, Joseph has been found wanting in propriety; in this lesser unveiling it is sufficient for Sir Oliver to arrive at the truth quickly. This scene was originally drafted to be played before the screen scene, but Sheridan would not have wished to detract from the dramatic impact of the latter.

## 5.2 THE DERIVATION OF THE PLOT

In a number of respects the plot is derivatory. Sheridan employs two traditional dramatic devices which are as old as comedy itself: characters in concealment overhear information which changes their attitudes to other people, and a disguised character tests the reactions of his relations to himself and to his notions of virtue. Sheridan, too, picks from the plots of his fellow dramatists. Six years earlier Samuel Foote had written *The Maid of Bath* in which one of the central figures is Solomon Teazle, an elderly man recently married to a young bride. His sentiments are much the same as those of Sir Peter: 'For my part, I can't see what pleasure pretty Misses can take in galloping to plays, and to balls, and to such expensive vagaries.' Furthermore, one can find echoes of a play by Molière (1622-73), *L'Ecole des Femmes*, of the comedies of Congreve which Sheridan admired, especially *The Way of the World*, and of the contemporary comedy *Know Your Own Mind* by Arthur Murphy (1727-1805). The artistry of Sheridan lies in the seemingly effortless construction of his intricate plot, not in its originality, which would seem in the eighteenth century to be an unusual virtue to rate highly.

## 5.3 THE LANGUAGE OF THE PLAY

**Words before characters**
Thomas Moore quotes Sheridan's opening scraps of dialogue from 'The Slanderers'. The words are unattached to speakers; they simply exist as amusing sayings:

> She is a constant attendant at church, and very frequently takes Dr M. Brawn home with her. . .

> I hate to repeat what I hear. . .

"She had twins", - How ill-natured! as I hope to be ma'am, she had but one! and that a little starved brat not worth mentioning.

Such jottings suggest snippets overheard in crowded assembly places. To these, Sheridan adds his own epigrams, which are pointed and often malicious, but still without apportioning them to characters:

> . . .ma'am, the match is certainly broke - no creature knows the cause; some say a flaw in the lady's character, and others, in the gentleman's fortune. . .

> The most intrepid blush; - I've known her complexion stand fire for an hour together.

Already we gain an impression that Sheridan is more interested in words and their bite than in the development of a character through the dialogue he speaks. Throughout the play the voice of Sheridan, rather than that of his characters, is heard. The playwright goes so far as to remove a character from his dialogue, substituting another to speak the same lines, with the expected result that this gives an inconsistency of character. An example is seen in the draft section 'Sir Peter Teazle' in which Sir Oliver, disguised as Mr Stanley, arrives at Joseph Surface's house and engages in an amusing conversation about Joseph's nerves with a servant. The humour lies in the irony beneath the servant's meaning: '. . .they say [Charity] begins at home - but my master is of that domestic sort that never stirs abroad at all.' When the drama is staged, it is Rowley who is given the task of commenting on Joseph's state; honest Rowley, a grave man, momentarily develops into a witty and amusing one. The change in the man is caused by the reallocation of the dialogue.

## Language and character

But there are some characters in whose language Sheridan takes a keen interest, making it a careful expression of their inner life. Joseph Surface speaks in elaborate and lengthy sentences, often employing aphorisms within the structure. Of his brother he says: 'I wish it were in my power to be of any essential service to him, for the man who does not share in the distresses of a brother, even though merited by his own misconduct, deserves. . .' (1.1). And usually, as here, this elaborate form enshrines a sententious comment, which draws the remark from those who admire Joseph that here is a man of sentiment. These qualities make a conversation with Joseph difficult, a point which Sheridan admirably illustrates in the proposal Joseph makes to Lady Teazle in the first part of the screen scene. Joseph takes each of Lady Teazle's protestations and elaborates it into a miniature argument in his own favour. Furthermore, he engages in rhetoric on behalf of both parties, allowing Lady Teazle (herself rarely at a loss for words) no part to play in the conversation. Taking up her remark about her innocence, he immediately makes a formal speech:

> 'Tis this very conscious innocence that is of the greatest prejudice to you. What is it makes you negligent of forms, and careless of the world's opinions? Why, the consciousness of your own innocence. What makes you thoughtless in your conduct, and apt to run into a thousand little imprudences? Why the consciousness of your own innocence. What makes you impatient of Sir Peter's temper, and outrageous at his suspicions? Why, the consciousness of your innocence. (4.1)

Mrs Candour is another hypocritical character, and this trait affects her speech, too. She also weaves aphorisms into her conversations, although they tend to be trite: 'Tale-bearers are as bad as the tale-makers – 'tis an old observation, and a very true one.' (1.1). She also uses rhetorical questions to introduce further scandal: 'How will you prevent people from talking? Today Mrs Clackitt assured me Mr and Mrs Honeymoon. . .'. Her sentences abound with names, which, when she reaches the height of the pace of her delivery, become just listings: 'Everybody almost is in the same way – Lord Spindle, Sir Thomas Splint, Captain Quinze and Mr Nickit.'

The interchanges of the Teazles present us with two patterns of speech. In spite of her rural origin, there is nothing rustic in Lady Teazle's speeches; they are polished and witty. When taken to task by her husband, her first instinct is to mimic the pattern of his phrases:

> SIR PETER  Lady Teazle, Lady Teazle, I'll not bear it!
> LADY TEAZLE  Sir Peter, Sir Peter, you may bear it or not as you please! (2.2)

Sometimes she wittily rebuffs the archaic sentiments of her husband:

> SIR PETER  So a husband is to have no influence, no authority?
> LADY TEAZLE  Authority, no to be sure. If you wanted authority over me, you should have adopted me and not married me.

A continuity in the delivery is gained by picking up a key word of the former speech, a mannerism both characters engage in:

> SIR PETER  . . .I'll not be ruined by your extravagance.
> LADY TEAZLE  My extravagance! I'm sure I'm not more extravagant than a woman of fashion ought to be.

In addition to his reactionary sentiments, which suggest he is of an older generation, Sir Peter uses a number of interjections, in themselves suggesting age: 'Slife', 'Oons' and 'Zounds' are examples from the argument in the second act.

The relationship of dialogue to character is considered approvingly by a writer (possibly David Garrick) in the *St James' Chronicle*: 'If *Dialogue* replete with Wit, yet as easy and natural as if there were none, and if that Wit, by being unaffected, is subservient to the character, be the true Conversation of Comedy, Mr Sheridan is most happy in that part of the Drama.' Now we have already noted that the dialogue is epigrammatic, and therefore artificial, and that Sheridan is often more interested in the expression of a sentiment than in discovering the true voice of a character: how does this square with the critic's remarks? The explanation lies in the assumption that a greater degree of artifice was expected on the eighteenth-century stage than we would find in a modern comedy. Many of the characters, too, are uttering sentiments, aphorisms and epigrams, and it is the wit of these (although it was sometimes felt that Sheridan's wit-traps were over-baited for the sake of gaining applause) which earns approbation.

## Irony

The twin disguises of Sir Oliver lead to situations in which ironic remarks are made. When, as Mr Premium, he visits Charles, Sir Oliver enquires about the subject of one of the paintings. 'What,' asks Charles, 'that ill-looking little fellow over the settee?' (4.1). The audience shares Sir Oliver's secret, whereas Charles, in his ignorance of this fact, is liable to make remarks about his uncle which are termed ironic. Careless enters into the conversation, ironically claiming that the likeness of Sir Oliver has 'an unforgiving eye and a damned disinheriting countenance', qualities which Sir Oliver, justly, is quick to repudiate. Similar situations occur in Sir Oliver's encounter, under the guise of Mr Stanley, with Joseph Surface. There is irony in Joseph's sententious reply to the claimant for charity: 'To pity without the power to relieve is still more painful than to ask and be denied.' (5.1). We can forecast at this point in the play that it will be ultimately to Joseph's financial detriment to refuse to aid Stanley.

Remarks made whilst in the hearing of a hidden person are capable of assuming an ironic colouring. Whilst Lady Teazle is hidden behind the screen in Joseph's library her husband examines the front of it, decorated with maps, and remarks, 'you make even your screen a source of knowledge' (4.3). The full implication of this ironic remark is not perceived at the time by the audience for it is only later that the slanderers seize on the information of the discovery of Lady Teazle and, in a wildly exaggerated form, offer it as 'knowledge' amongst the gossips of the town. Sir Peter's subsequent unburdening of his doubts about Lady Teazle's faithfulness to himself, and her imagined intrigue with Charles Surface, take on an ironic tone as the husband pours out his doubts to the very person who is attempting to cuckold him.

## Imagery

A number of images run through the play. The title of the play presents the deliberately inappropriate metaphor of a college for the slanderers and their gossip. Their attention is continually brought to bear on the technique of spreading malice, and it is this which forms the skill of the academy: 'The malice of a good thing, is the barb that makes it stick,' (1.1) remarks Lady Sneelwell. The factual acquisitions of their learning are the scraps of news, true or false, which the members of the academy can share amongst themselves and pass to the outside world to the consternation or delight of society. At the conclusion of the play, the metaphor is neatly wrapped up: 'Lady Teazle, licentiate, begs leave to return the diploma' (5.3). A state of true tutelage is expressed by Charles in declaring that Maria will be his 'monitor', his 'gentle guide'.

It is not only the collective relationship of the slanderers for which an academic metaphor is employed. The relationship which exists between Lady Teazle and Joseph, once the young lady has been inveigled to Joseph's library, is that of a pupil and her master. Although the metaphor is not overtly stated, the didactic nature of Joseph's utterances makes this relationship clear: 'When a husband entertains a groundless suspicion of his wife and withdraws his confidence from her, the original compact is broken' (4.3).

A further metaphor of contempt for the slanderers and their misguided behaviour is that of the making of counterfeit currency. Sir Peter expresses this tersely: 'these utterers of forged tales, coiners of scandal and clippers of reputation' (2.1). F. W. Bateson points out that these activities are the work of 'the abusers of monetary system – those who put forged coins into circulation, those responsible for the actual forgery, those who debase currency values by cutting away coins' outer rim'. Later, Sir Peter suggests a just retribution for slanderers, couching his sentiments in terms of banking: '. . .in all cases of slander currency, whenever the drawer of the lie was not to be found, the injured parties should have a right to come on any of the endorsers' (2.2).

Family affection is often viewed in terms of hard cash. Whilst she is hidden behind the screen, Lady Teazle hears her husband express his intention of allowing her an annuity of eight hundred pounds a year, as well as his fortune at his death. It is this financial consideration for his wife which impinges on Lady Teazle's conscience, as she realises her husband's consideration for her. In the same vein, Sir Oliver's affection for his nephews is shown in his settlements and the demands he makes of them in his disguises. Sheridan is a realist: the bribing of Snake reminds the audience that even the virtue of truthfulness can be bought at a price, and as by money Lady Teazle recognises her husband's affection for her, so by money the imputation of slander is shown to be a forgery.

The important role that money plays in the fashionable town life is stressed in these harsh financial images.

## Speaking to the audience

In these considerations of the language of the play we have concentrated on the exchanges of the characters amongst themselves. A further consideration is the direct address to the audience which some of the characters employ. Less direct communication with the spectators is made in *The School for Scandal* than in many plays of Sheridan's day, but nevertheless, soliloquies and asides occur. The longest direct speech in the play is made by Sir Peter in the second scene. In this he engages the audience by asking a question, 'When an old bachelor marries a young wife, what is he to expect?' upon which he expatiates by way of an answer. Instead of introducing Lady Teazle, the subject of Sir Peter's speech, immediately afterwards, Sheridan brings on Rowley so that together they may converse about her. The audience has to wait until the next scene before it can witness the confrontation between husband and wife. Having established Sir Peter as a link with the audience, Sheridan continues to use him as such, and on several occasions he emphasises his feelings by a few words of direct address. However, Sir Peter is not the only person to do this. Joseph also engages in the convention: a strange choice, for the audience is alienated from him as soon as it discovers that character's lack of sincerity. Charles, at the end of the play, addresses rhymed couplets to the audience, asking for its approbation of the piece.

An unusual application of the convention of direct address occurs near the beginning of the screen scene. Joseph is left on stage alone and ruminates on the care with which he must proceed in his intrigue with Lady Teazle. On entering through the proscenium doors she notices he is speaking and remarks: 'What! Sentiment in soliloquy now?' (4.3). It was a Restoration convention that soliloquies could be overheard by the actors, but with the increasing realism of eighteenth-century drama, the practice was condemned. Here is a half-way point: Lady Teazle is aware that a speech is in progress but she does not catch the drift of it.

The aside is a much briefer form of address to the audience which Sheridan uses occasionally in the play. In the auction scene Sir Oliver makes a number of asides to the audience emphasising the humour and irony of a situation. Typical is his remark about Charles suggesting a selling price of ten pounds for the portrait of Sir Richard Raveline: 'Heaven deliver me! His famous uncle Richard for ten pounds!' (4.1).

Later in the play, in the screen scene, Joseph, too, indulges in a number of asides. These are without ironical comment, however, and merely stress the dangers Joseph is in as he plays the amorous game of hide-and-seek with Lady Teazle and Sir Peter.

**Metre, verse and song**

The final consideration in this section is of Sheridan's use of verse and song in his comedy. The greater part of the text is in prose. Much of it is artificial, carefully balanced, and rhythmic. As an example, one may notice Sir Peter's sentence describing his wife: 'Yet with what a charming air she contradicts everything I say – and how pleasingly she shows her contempt for my authority.' Each half of the sentence patterns the other in its construction. Hidden within the prose, too, are numbers of iambic feet:

. . ./with what/ a charm/ing air/she con/tradicts/ ever/y thing/ I say/

Sheridan was conscious of these, and expected his performers to stress the strong beats. Later, when rehearsals for *Pizarro* were under way, he would sit in a side-box hammering the rhythm of these iambs on the ledge.

It is left to Sir Benjamin Backbite to introduce some verse into the comedy. To Lady Sneerwell's circle he presents his 'epigram' on Lady Betty Curricle's horses. For this verse Sheridan simply lifted some lines written by himself in 1776 on 'A Lady of Fashion'. Since the Renaissance scholarly writers had established their claim to rank among the wits by penning a brief rhymed epigram (an ingenious point expressed in verse), but that by Backbite is hardly witty or scholarly, as it simply compared the legs of the horses to those of a macaroni or fop.

The three rhymed couplets at the end of the last act conveniently signal the play's conclusion; unfortunately they are feeble and unworthy of the rest of the dialogue which is sharply aimed and witty in its precision.

Only one song occurs by way of musical interlude, and this is unusually sparse for an eighteenth-century comedy. As in Oliver Goldsmith's earlier play it is within the context of a drinking scene. In various manuscripts of *The School for Scandal* is about the behaviour of people; therefore the some resemblances to a song in a play by Sir John Suckling (1609-42), *The Goblins*, and may well be a paraphrase.

## 5.4 THE PRINCIPAL CHARACTERS

*The School for Scandal* is about the behaviour of people; therefore the playwright's delineation of each character must be precise and true. For Sheridan it was a great advantage that, before he began to write the play, he knew the company at Drury Lane, a group of performers who had been chosen and trained by David Garrick. Once Sheridan had conceived the main roles in his comedy and decided on the cast, he used each performer as a working model for that character. Therefore, in these notes it will not be inappropriate to consider the originator of each role in addition to the part itself.

## Lady Teazle

Shortly before the play opens, Lady Teazle had married Sir Peter Teazle. She is a young, vivacious girl from the country, he an elderly town bachelor. Lady Teazle's life in the country seems to have been uneventful: she is the daughter of 'a plain country squire' (2.1), used to such jobs as housekeeping ('a bunch of keys at your side'), embroidery, inspecting the dairy, and looking after the poultry. Her evening recreations consisted of no more than playing cards with the village curate, reading sermons to her aunt, or playing melodies on the spinet.

In London, Lady Teazle's life becomes dominated by fashion. The obvious displays of this are in her clothes and the flowers with which the Teazle household is decorated. It is fashionable to belong to a clique which engages in gossip and slander: hence Lady Teazle's admittance into Lady Sneerwell's circle. It is fashionable, too, to be seen with a lover; but restraint allows Lady Teazle to admit Joseph Surface 'no further than fashion requires' (2.2). She does, however, stay faithful to her husband, in spite of Joseph's jibe that her idea of honourableness is an ill consequence of her 'country education' (4.3). Alongside this flirtation she is reputed to be the mistress of Charles Surface, an unfounded rumour spread by Mrs Candour.

The intrinsic honourableness of Lady Teazle is revealed when her husband discovers her hiding behind the screen in Joseph's house. She confesses to her husband that she has been 'seduced by [Joseph's] insidious arguments'. Her repentance and charm eventually disperse Sir Peter's suspicions, and hope for the future is expressed in Sir Peter's toast to Maria and Charles: '. . .may you live as happily together as Lady Teazle and I intend to do!' (5.3). As she forsakes the fashionableness of admitting to a lover, so Lady Teazle also renounces her membership of Lady Sneerwell's 'scandalous college', resolving that no longer will she be a detractor of character.

Two dramatic conventions fuse in the character of Lady Teazle; that of the young wife who marries an elderly husband and that of the country-woman who is transported to the town; the first of these conventions stems back to Roman comedy. The situation obviously is one designed to cause jealousy, and one of which any unscrupulous young male may attempt to take advantage. The second convention, the countrywoman arrived in town, was often exploited in Restoration comedy, for example in *The Country Wife* by William Wycherley. In this, Pinchwife, who has occasion to come to London for the marriage of his sister, Alithea, brings with him from the country his young wife, Margery. Highly jealous for his wife's honour, Pinchwife soon puts ideas into Margery's head. In many respects this situation is parallel to the one in which the Teazles find themselves.

The part of Lady Teazle was taken by Mrs Frances Abington (1737?-1815). In January 1777, a malicious article on this actress, illustrated by a silhouette of her, appeared in the *Town and Country Magazine*, the periodical which Sheridan mentions in the first act of the play. By the date of the first performance Mrs Abingdon was at least forty, but the charm of her artistry made her performance credible. Her voice was high in pitch, suggesting girlishness, and, said an eyewitness, her articulation was so precise 'that every syllable she utters is conveyed distinctly, and even harmoniously'. Many watching the comedy would be aware that Mrs Abington was the mistress of the Earl of Shelburne; her part in the play offered an ironic contrast with her off-stage activities.

### Sir Peter Teazle

Sir Peter is Lady Teazle's 56-year-old husband. The overall impression the audience gains of him is of a man of honour. He is pompous, opinionated, tetchy, but nevertheless his uprightness of character helps him to pass unscathed through the situation of the play.

Sheridan presents his audience with a stock character: the elderly bachelor who marries a young wife had often been witnessed on stage prior to Sir Peter's entry; the appointed guardian of two brothers of contrasting virtue was not a new role. And yet into this stock character Sheridan fuses humour and a humanity which gains the affection of the audience. We view Teazle principally with regard to his relationship with his wife. His first words to the audience stress the dramatic conventionality of the situation he finds himself in: 'When an old bachelor marries a young wife, what is he to expect?' (1.2). In the following scene the difficulties he endures are shown to the audience when Lady Teazle makes her husband the butt of her witty sallies. On his complaint of her extravagance in buying flowers she immediately turns the argument on her husband:

> Lord, Sir Peter, am I to blame because flowers are dear in cold weather? You should find fault with the climate and not with me. (2.1)

In spite of his wife's provocations, Sir Peter is always a realist and possesses an underlying stability which his tetchiness would seem to belie. He assures his wife: '. . . though your conduct may disturb my peace, it shall never break my heart, I promise you'. Later in the play, when his wife is discovered hiding in Joseph's house, after Sir Peter's opening expletive, 'Lady Teazle, by all that's damnable!' a keenness to arrive at the truth prompts him to listen rather than speak. Rowley easily persuades Sir Peter to follow his advice and become reconciled to Lady Teazle. Sir Peter's penultimate speech in the play looks forward hopefully to a deepening of understanding between himself and Lady Teazle. When we compare this speech to Sir Peter's first in the play, we realise that his relationship with his wife has developed. No other person exemplifies a like maturation.

We must consider Sir Peter's dealings with the Surface family and with Lady Sneerwell's circle. Sir Oliver Surface has been a long-standing friend of Sir Peter's, and on going abroad to live, he made Sir Peter the guardian of his two nephews, Charles and Joseph. This, together with his guardianship of Maria, is another mark of the trustworthiness of the man. As with many elderly cronies (one thinks of the friendship of Hardcastle and Sir Charles Marlow in *She Stoops to Conquer*) the affection between Sir Peter and Sir Oliver remains unaffected by time and circumstance.

Sir Peter is opinionated. He polarises his attitude towards the brothers: Charles is a profligate and Joseph a model of virtue, and until the end of Act 4 no action of either brother will make him less inflexible. When the screen falls and the truth is out, his remonstration to Joseph is contained in a single sentence: Joseph is a villain who is to be left to his own conscience. In the final scene of the play, which is in the nature of a tribunal, Sir Peter reiterates his findings about Joseph: he is 'mean, treacherous and hypocritical'. To the end Sir Peter continues to address Charles as 'rogue' – but there is a change of tone in his use of the appellation.

Sir Peter views Lady Sneerwell and her friends with horror. He spends little time in this company, although his wife frequents it. In the course of his only attendance he attempts to remonstrate with Lady Sneerwell: '...true wit is more nearly allied to good nature than your ladyship is aware of' (2.2). When he sees his words are without effect he leaves – but in doing so makes one of his memorable remarks: 'But I leave my character behind me'. In the last act the principal members of the scandal academy invade the Teazle house, bringing with them a series of unsubstantiated rumours about Sit Peter's engagement in a duel. Sir Peter, without circumlocution, hurls the truth at the gaggle of malicious gossips: 'Fiends! Vipers! Furies! Oh, that their own venom would choke them!' (5.2). In his relationships with his wife, the Surface family and the slanderers, Sir Peter is used as a link character, drawing the various strands of the comedy together.

This challenging character role was originally played by Thomas King (1730-1805), who was an established comedian in the Drury Lane company. The critic William Hazlitt has left a brief description of King in action:

> King, whose acting left a taste on the palate, sharp and sweet like a quince; with an old, hard, rough, withered face, like a John-apple, puckered up into a thousand wrinkles; with shrewd hints and tart replies; 'with nods and becks and wreathed smiles'; who was the real amorous, wheedling, or hasty, choleric, peromptory old gentleman in Sir Peter Teazle. . .

## Joseph Surface

The play allows the audience to view Joseph Surface in a number of contexts: Joseph the mean and rapacious; Joseph the seducer; and Joseph the man of sentiment. Joseph's meanness is dramatically illustrated in his encounter with his uncle, Sir Oliver Surface, in the guise of Mr Stanley, a poor relation. At once Joseph addresses the unwelcome visitor in sententious terms: 'He that is in distress, though a stranger, has a right to claim kindred with the wealthy' (5.1). Immediately, however, he disclaims that he himself is able to offer help: 'I am sure I wish I was of that class and had it in my power to offer you even a small relief.' The audience has already been informed that Sir Oliver had bestowed twelve thousand pounds on his nephew, and it also knows of the scant financial help that Joseph has given Charles. Nevertheless, Joseph takes his hypocrisy further: '. . .you have heard, I doubt not, of the extravagance of my brother. There are very few would credit what I have done for that unfortunate young man.' He is adamant in his refusal to help his uncle.

This scene is carefully placed. The audience has already witnessed Sir Oliver's visit to Charles, disguised as Premium, and noted the pleasurable outcome for both parties of that encounter. It has seen, too, the disgracing of Joseph in the library scene. Now it is presented with the final undoing of Joseph brought about by his failure to recognise his uncle (in eighteenth-century dramas the discerning often perceive family relationships) and by his failure to put his money to good use in almsgiving.

By the time the audience is made aware of the role of Joseph as a romantic wooer, it has already discovered that his pose as a man of sentiment is mere pretence and, since his apparent love for Lady Sneerwell is recognised as a blind, it instantly suspects Joseph's intentions in any further affair. In rapid succession spectators are shown Joseph's wooing of Maria and, when he has descended to his knees and thus been discovered by Lady Teazle, the beginnings of his proposal to the latter which is continued later in his library. He lures Lady Teazle to his house, explaining that their relationship is to be one of a married woman and her *cicisbeo* – a recognised companion and gallant. Once Lady Teazle is in the library Joseph attempts to apply sophistry in order to seduce her; at first he states that Sir Peter's worries about her faithfulness dissolve the matrimonial contract; and then he suggests that if Lady Teazle would make 'a trifling *faux-pas*' 'all scandal would cease at once' (4.3).

When Lady Teazle is discovered by her husband hiding in the library, Joseph's lack of gallantry reveals the true man: a lame excuse for his conduct is followed by an assertion that Lady Teazle is mad. He is sure that his downfall is due not to himself but to fate: '. . .Fortune never played a man of my policy such a trick before' (5.1). Joseph is an example of the unrelenting villain. A character such as Sir Peter matures as the play proceeds, but no change of sentiment or moral improvement occurs in Joseph; he remains constant so that on his final exit Sir Peter can make his ironic remark: 'Moral to the last drop' (5.3). His is a rigidly enclosed, self-serving nature, and so it remains.

Joseph is seen as the 'Man of Sentiment'. The eighteenth-century concept of sentiment is dealt with in Section 4.3. Sufficient here to point out that a true man of sentiment is open to the experiences which surround him and is continually making responses to these, whether they present themselves in the form of natural phenomena, the arts or people. Unlike most men of sentiment, Joseph betrays no response to nature, nor is any appreciation of such arts as painting or poetry in evidence. He does, however, come into contact with people, and his response is to shy away from any expression of feeling; instead he rebuffs other people's approaches with a witty, epigrammatic turn of phrase or an ironic platitude: 'Ah, Mrs Candour, if everybody had your forbearance and good nature!' (1.1). He is so much the opposite of the man of sentiment that his utterances on the subject are ironic comments.

John Palmer (1742-98), who played the part of Joseph Surface, resembled him in his hypocrisy and his plausibility. Palmer was nicknamed 'Plausible Jack', and it is perhaps more than coincidental that Sheridan, in early drafts of the play, names the character Plausible. He was an idle and unscrupulous fellow, highly attractive to women and always acting, in true life, as a man of superior accomplishments. Charles Lamb described Palmer's vocal delivery:

> Jack had two voices, – both plausible, hypocritical, and insinuating; but his secondary or supplemental voice [was] still more decisively histrionic than his common one. ... The...*sentiments* in Joseph Surface were thus marked out in a sort of italics to the audience.

### Charles Surface

Of the faculties needed for the role of Charles Surface, the essayist William Hazlitt wrote: 'A good face and figure, easy manners, evident good nature, animation and sensibility'. The two brothers are a contrast: as Joseph Surface is the withdrawn hypocrite, so Charles is the good-natured man, a type much admired in the eighteenth-century. The comparison which Sheridan makes of the two men may be modelled on the drawing of Tom Jones, the title hero of the novel by Joseph Fielding (1707-54), and of his brother Blifil. Although Tom is a lusty fellow who loves too well, in his presence people find both a sense of fun and their own fulfilment. Acquaintance with Blifil, however, tends to diminish people. So it is with Charles Surface: he is wildly extravagant, intemperate, loves the society of women, yet his is a natural, open personality and he has a capacity for affection and generosity towards which others can respond. He is, too, a benevolent person, and it is this virtue which prompts him to keep his benefactor uncle's portrait rather than sell it to Mr Premium. There is, of course, room for reformation, and Rowley, in quoting a description of Prince Hal in *Henry IV*, acknowledges this:

> . . .you will find in the younger brother one who, in the midst of folly and dissipation, has still, as our immortal bard expresses it, 'a tear for pity and a hand open as day for melting charity' (3.1)

Yet, in choosing a quotation describing Hal, Rowley is also making a prognostication that eventually 'folly and dissipation' will give way to a mature lifestyle.

For the space of three acts the audience learns much about Charles solely by hearsay. Spectators are thus able to form their own idea of this attractive rapscallion. It transpires that he is loved in the first place by Lady Sneerwell in spite of the fact that she, in common with others, regards him as 'that libertine, that extravagant, that bankrupt in fortune and reputation' (1.1). Lady Sneerwell knows that Charles and Maria, Sir Peter Teazle's ward, love each other. The first sight of Charles the audience enjoys is at a drinking party in his own house, a carousing affair in which the praises of wine and women – Maria in particular – are sung.

After this the meeting with his uncle, Sir Oliver, disguised as Mr Premium, takes place. Charles has little sense of heritage: for him the collection in the picture gallery is as dead wood holding no sentimental appeal and can be sold in order to raise cash. Sir Oliver's expostulation has no effect on Charles: 'Odd's life, do you take me for Shylock in the play that you would raise money of me on your own flesh and blood?' (3.3); the young man replies with a further question: 'When a man wants money, where the plague should he get assistance if he can't make free with his own relations?' In the auction scene one realises that Charles' behaviour is outrageous, and yet it is done with panache (especially in his use of genealogy as both catalogue and auctioneer's hammer) and with such a sense of fun that the audience shares Sir Oliver's mixed feelings of horror at Charles' audacity but affection for his person. It is Charles who acknowledges, as Joseph denies: 'The old fellow [Sir Oliver] has been very good to me. . .' (4.1) and on his nephew's refusal to sell the portrait of Sir Oliver, his uncle sums up the young man's qualities in his punning invocation: 'A dear extravagant rogue!' Yet Charles denies himself all of the money gained from the sale and his first act is to get Rowley to deliver one hundred pounds to Mr Stanley, an action Rowley finds imprudent. Again, Charles is able to defend his position with a witty epigram, rather than with one of Joseph's sententious aphorisms: '. . .Justice is an old lame hobbling beldame, and I can't get her to keep pace with Generosity for the soul of me.'

Charles, it has been noted, is an open person with few secrets of his own; indeed, he uncovers the secrets of others. As soon as he learns that Sir Peter is closeted in Joseph's library, he pulls him into the open. It is Charles, too, who, on hearing of the French milliner in hiding, wishes to see her and topples the screen, so revealing Lady Teazle.

Described by Charles Churchill (1731-64) in *The Rosciad* 'the genteel, the airy and the smart', William Smith (1730-1819), popularly known as 'Gentleman' Smith, took the part of Charles Surface. Possibly his aristocratic bearing was the result of an education at Eton College and Cambridge University.

The *London Magazine* praised the performance: 'Mr Smith's Charles was one of the most genuine, easy, natural, and elegantly played characters we have seen in a new comedy for some years.'

## Sir Oliver Surface

Sir Oliver Surface embodies two stock types common in eighteenth-century comedy - he is, in the words of Cecil Price, 'the absent relative and the disguised watcher'. Of the first of these roles we know little. Crabtree simply remarks to Joseph: 'He has been in the East Indies a long time. You can scarcely remember him, I believe?' (1.1). As an expatriate, he took a lively interest in his two nephews and, although Sir Peter had been appointed their guardian, 'Sir Oliver's eastern liberality gave them an early independence' (1.2). Fifteen years earlier, whilst living in England, Sir Oliver had been the bosom friend of Sir Peter: 'We have had many a day together,' says Teazle, and goes on to describe, somewhat wistfully we feel, how they used 'to rail at matrimony together'. Sir Oliver had remained a bachelor; not so Sir Peter.

We may be tempted to ask what Sir Oliver was doing in the East Indies. A possibility is that he served as an official of the East India Company, an association of merchants engaged in trade. Here was one way in which he would have rapidly acquired considerable sums of money and thus gained the term 'nabob'. If this suggestion was also in Sheridan's mind, it would account for the hale condition of Sir Oliver, for in the Indian climate only a healthy third of the English traders survived the tropical diseases.

The convention of the disguised watcher was already established on the Georgian stage. Many such observers of society could trace the convention's origin to the Duke of Vienna in Shakespeare's *Measure for Measure*. Sheridan was probably aware of a more recent example in the sentimental comedy of *The West Indian* by Richard Cumberland in which Stockwell, the father of Belcour, is secretly watching his son's progress in London. In order to observe carefully the responses of his nephews, Sir Oliver plays two roles: Mr Premium and Mr Stanley. Mr Premium is the successful broker, thrust, to his surprise, into a situation in which he is asked to buy his family's portraits. Mr Stanley strikes the opposite note: a poor relation, who finds neither alms nor hospitality at Joseph's door.

In the winding up of the plot Sir Oliver is seen both as judge, in his condemnation of Joseph, and as benign and paternalistic in arranging the marriage of Maria and Charles.

Richard Yates (1706?-1796) took the role of Sir Oliver Surface. He was a bluff, elderly actor, and we gain an impression of how he played his part from a description of his acting by the Anglo-Irish playwright John O'Keeffe (1747-1833): 'His manner was of the dry or grave humour, but perfectly natural; his speech slow; he knew he had his audience, and therefore took them at his leisure.'

## Maria

The role of Maria ia an insignificant one. She is the prize for whom Charles and Joseph Surface compete; but in her own right she is neither a strongly drawn, nor a lively, character. She lacks the waywardness, as well as the sparkle, of Lady Teazle; instead, we see in her an example of dutiful worthiness. Maria is a girl of integrity. Although surrounded by the circle of gossips, she refuses to join their slanderous detractions: '. . .wit loses its respect with me when I see it in company with malice' (1.1). She also abominates her lover, Sir Benjamin Backbite, as his conversation is 'a perpetual libel on all his acquaintance'. Furthermore she finds slander in a man 'contemptible'. People attempt to damage Maria's relationship with Charles. She is forbidden by her guardian, Sir Peter Teazle, to see him or to correspond; Joseph Surface and Lady Sneerwell threaten the 'mutual attachment' of the couple; and at one stage Maria, hearing gossip about Charles, thinks that he is unworthy of her love.

The role was originally written for Mary Robinson (1758-1800). However, at the time she was pregnant. In her place Priscilla Hopkins (1756-1845), the daughter of the Drury Lane stage manager, took the part. She was a pretty girl, but, slight though the part is, she could not do justice to it. Of her performance the London Magazine noted: 'Neither her stile [sic] of playing, dress or person, seemed fully to convey the portrait the author intended to lay before the public.'

## Lady Sneerwell

Most of the gossips remain detached from the plot of this comedy. Lady Sneerwell is the exception. In the opening scene of the play, set in her house, she introduces themes which run through the play. Firstly, Lady Sneerwell informs the audience (and Snake) that Joseph is a hypocrite. Secondly, she is determined to break the affection of Charles for Maria, for, although she accepts him as 'that libertine', she is herself in love with him.

Lady Sneerwell is aptly called the president of the 'scandalous college' (5.3) by Lady Teazle; she attempts a justification for her slanderous talk: early in her life she was wounded by its 'envenomed tongue' (1.1); but even so, she takes great pleasure in reducing others 'to the level of [her] own injured reputation'. It has to be admitted that there is wit in her strictures of others, and she is not without recognising this: 'The malice of a good thing is the barb that makes it stick.' However the later remarks of Mrs Candour, and even of Lady Teazle, are more malicious, causing Lady Sneerwell to utter a remonstrance: 'I see you can be a little severe' (2.2).

At the end of the play Lady Sneerwell is most undignified. She is betrayed by Snake; the town knows of her love for Charles and of the forged letters allegedly from Charles to Lady Teazle. Angrily she makes her last curse: 'May your husband live these fifty years' (5.3). Others on the stage at the time summarise her character as a 'Fury' and a 'malicious creature'.

## Mrs Candour

The dictionary of Dr Samuel Johnson (1709-84), published in 1755, defined candour as a virtue. By 1798 George Canning could pray, 'Save, save, oh, save me from the Candid Friend'. In Mrs Candour we find both of these connotions reflected: she constantly claims that she is benignly defending her friends, and yet she belies the claim by repeating all manner of gossip.

The character is described before she appears on stage. Lady Sneerwell says she is a 'little talkative'; Maria, more correctly, refers to her 'gross affectation of good nature and benevolence'; and Joseph caps this by his observation: 'Whenever I hear the current running against the character of my friends, I never think them in such danger as when Candour undertakes their defence' (1.1). Her first words to Maria harp on the supposed rift between her and Charles, as well as on an estrangement between Sir Peter and Lady Teazle. This is a clue to her method of working: her remarks spread a plague of destructiveness. There are sexual overtones to many of her remarks, whether she is describing assignations or pregnancies.

Although Mrs Candour has a carriage, a symbol of some status in society, the impression is given that her social status differs from that of Lady Sneerwell. Mrs Candour is attempting to buy her way into society with the coinage of malicious gossip and it is to her advantage to make sure that it is newly minted. 'We shall have the whole affair,' she says, speaking of Lady Teazle's discovery behind the screen, 'in the newspapers with the names of the parties at length before I have dropped the story at a dozen houses' (5.2).

The actress who first played the part, Miss Jane Pope (1742-1818), spoke her lines in so natural a tone of voice, said the critic Leigh Hunt

(1784-1859), that it hid the affected sentiments she spoke. The result was a highly convincing characterisation, highlighting the ironic implications in the disparity between the appearance of Mrs Candour's concern and the reality of her malice.

## Rowley

Rowley had been steward to Charles and Joseph Surface's late father; at the time of the play he is steward to Sir Oliver Surface. He is a man of integrity, perspicacious and resourceful, and as such mirrors the Restoration tradition of the honest steward. He serves two principal functions: he is the confidant of Sir Peter Teazle and as such helps to reconcile Lady Teazle to her husband near the end of the play; and he advises both Sir Peter and Sir Oliver Surface on the true merits of the Surface brothers. With the latter he sets in motion the two interludes in which Sir Oliver appears as Mr Premium at Sir Peter's instigation and Mr Stanley at Rowley's own suggestion. Thus the steward is an important factor in the development of the plot. His skill in setting events in motion is also apparent in his ability to unravel the intrigues of others. It is he who discovers that the letter Sir Peter found, ostensibly from Lady Teazle to Charles, was a forgery. In his speeches there is a quiet authority; he is able, for example, to remonstrate with Sir Peter when he wishes his wife to 'pine a little': 'Oh, this is ungenerous in you' (5.2).

It was natural that Sheridan should turn to James Aickin (?-1830) to play the part for, said the theatre historian, the Revd John Genest (1764-1839), 'his forte lay in the representation of an honest steward'.

## The changing cast

Character, situation and dialogue make a play. The strength of early performances of *The School for Scandal* lay in the combination of actor and character, a coalescence Sheridan was able to achieve as he wrote the play bearing his company in mind. Both Charles Lamb and James Boaden lamented the distancing from the original caused by the passing of time. Boaden wrote:

> I think his comedy was better *spoken*, in all its parts, than any play I have witnessed upon the stage. [Each change in the cast has caused] a sensible diminution of the original effect. The lingered sentiment of Palmer - the jovial smartness of Smith - the caustic shyness of King - the brilliant loquacity of Abington, - however congenial to the play, have long been silent. [But] the first actors of *The School for Scandal* were imitated throughout the country, and some portion of *their* [performance] must reach a distant age.

It is worth bearing this in mind when next watching the play!

# 6  AN EXAMINATION OF A SPECIMEN PASSAGE

## 6.1  SPECIMEN PASSAGE

LADY SNEERWELL  The Paragraphs you say, Mr. Snake, were all
inserted?

SNAKE  They were Madam - and as I copied them myself in a feign'd
Hand there can be no suspicion whence they came. -

LADY SNEER  Did you circulate the Report of Lady Brittle's Intrigue
with Captain Boastall?

SNAKE  That is in as fine a Train as your Ladyship could wish. -
In the common course of Things, I think it must reach Mrs.
Clackitt's Ears within four and twenty Hours and then you know
the Business is as good as done.                                                    10

LADY SNEER  Why truly Mrs. Clackitt has a very pretty Talent, and
a great deal of industry.

SNAKE  True, madam, and has been tolerably successful in her day.
To my Knowledge - she has been the cause of six matches being
broken off, and three sons being disinherited, of four forced
Elopements, as many close confinements, nine separate main-
tenances, and two Divorces. - nay, I have more than once traced
her causing a Tête-à-Tête in the Town and Country Magazine -
when the Parties perhaps have never seen each other's Faces before
in the course of their Lives.                                                         20

LADY SNEER  She certainly has Talents, but her manner is gross.

SNAKE  'Tis very true - she generally designs well - has a free tongue
and a bold invention - but her colouring is too dark and her
outline often extravagant. She wants that delicacy of Hint - and
mellowness of sneer which distinguish your Ladyship's Scandal.

LADY SNEER  Ah! you are Partial Snake.

SNAKE  Not in the least - everybody allows that Lady Sneerwell
can do more with a word or a Look, than many can with the most

labour'd Detail even when they happen to have a little truth on
their side to support it.                                        30

LADY SNEER  Yes my dear Snake, and I am no Hypocrite to deny
the satisfaction I reap from the Success of my Efforts – wounded
myself in the early Part of my Life by the envenom'd Tongue of
Slander I confess I have since known no Pleasure equal to the
reducing others, to the Level of my own injured Reputation – .

SNAKE  Nothing can be more natural – But Lady Sneerwell – There
is one affair in which you have lately employ'd me wherein I
confess I am at a Loss to guess your motives.

LADY SNEER  I conceive you mean with respect to my neighbour
Sir Peter Teazle and his Family?                                40

SNAKE  I do; here are two young men, to whom Sir Peter has acted
as a kind of Guardian since their Father's death, the elder possessing the most amiable Character and universally well spoken of,
the other the most dissipated and extravagant young Fellow in
the Kingdom without Friends or Character – the former an
avow'd Admirer of your Ladyship, and apparently your Favourite;
the latter attached to Maria, Sir Peter's ward – and confessedly
belov'd by her – now on the face of these circumstances it is
utterly unaccountable to me why you, the Widow of a City
Knight with a good Jointure – should not close with the Passion 50
of a man of such character and expectations as Mr. Surface – and
more so why you should be so uncommonly earnest to destroy
the mutual Attachment – subsisting between his brother Charles,
and Maria.

LADY SNEER  Then at once to unravel this mystery – I must inform
you that Love has no share whatever in the intercourse between
Mr. Surface and me.

SNAKE  No!

LADY SNEER  His real attachment is to Maria or her Fortune – but
finding in his Brother a favour'd Rival He has been obliged to 60
mask his Pretensions – and profit by my Assistance.

SNAKE  Yet still I am more puzzled why you should interest yourself in his Success –

LADY SNEER  Heav'ns! how full you are!, – cannot you surmise the
weakness which I hitherto thro' shame have conceal'd even from
you? – must I confess that Charles – that Libertine, that extravagant – that Bankrupt in Fortune and Reputation – that He it is
for whom I am thus anxious and malicious and to gain whom I
would sacrifice – everything?

SNAKE  Now indeed – your conduct appears consistent – but how 70
came you and Mr. Surface so confidential –

LADY SNEER  For our mutual interest; I have found him out a long time since - I know him to be artful selfish and malicious - in short, a Sentimental Knave.

SNAKE  Yet, Sir Peter vows He has not his equal in England - and above all - he praises him as a *Man of Sentiment* -

LADY SNEER  True and with the assistance of his Sentiments and Hypocrisy he has brought him entirely into his Interest with regard to Maria.   80


## 6.2 COMMENTARY

Sheridan uses Lady Sneerwell and Mr Snake to introduce many of the principal characters in the play and to give a certain amount of background information. Snake and Sneerwell are also used to set the tone of the play; they are two people who revel in the spread of slander. In Restoration comedies the slander of 'the Town' was spread by word of mouth; however, by the last quarter of the eighteenth century it was necessary to use newspapers to expedite the dissemination of false information and malice, as the opening remarks show. A seemingly chance remark of Lady Sneerwell's indirectly acts as a comment on her relation to Snake. She claims that in her youth she was damaged by the 'envenomed tongue of slander'. Now in her middle-age she uses the venomous and rightly named Snake as the disseminator of lies which she directs against society.

It is a strange ploy on the playwright's part to use these two characters, whose words cannot be trusted, to give information; the audience is expected to tune in with the convention that the people chosen to make the introductions in the first act of the play are to be regarded as reliable. In these early lines a trio who figure only as passing names are brought to the attention of the audience. In a single proper noun the characteristics of their subject is described: Lady Brittle and Captain Boastall are instantly comprehended; Mrs Clackitt's name descends from an obsolete French verb *clagueter*, meaning 'to chatter'. Other names later materialise as substantial characters: Lady Sneerwell makes reference to 'Sir Peter Teazle and his family', and Snake clarifies this remark, identifying Sir Peter's two wards, Joseph and Charles Surface. Here again the surnames indicate character: 'Teazle' - the prickly head of a plant used to 'tease' or raise up the nap on a cloth; and 'Surface' indicates the visible, superficial (and misjudged) characteristics of each of the brothers.

As we would expect, some of the major themes of the play are stated in this early section of the text. The following are noted here: the dissemination of scandal; the picture of a society governed by deceit and artifice; and the concepts of 'sentiment' and the 'sentimental'. Scandal, it has been said, is spread by means of print and the journal which Sheridan singles out is the *Town and Country Magazine*, a monthly periodical which was published from January 1769 until December 1797, a good run for a paper in the eighteenth century. The magazine gained some passing notoriety because of the inclusion of the section 'Tête-à-Tête' in which scandal in high society was exposed. Identification was made possible by the silhouettes which illustrated the articles and by the use of easily recognisable pseudonyms. Horace Walpole, for example, appeared as 'Baron Otranto', an allusion to his novel *The Castle of Otranto*. Snake flatters Lady Sneerwell when he comments on the economy with which she can achieve her malicious ends: '. . .Lady Sneerwell can do more with a word or a look than many can with the most laboured detail. . .'. This is but the beginning of that vice which appears throughout the comedy. The slanderers, headed by Lady Sneerwell, are a faction against which the virtuous characters have to contend.

The second theme the text introduces is that of artifice and deceit. We may presume that much scandal is false, but Snake exemplifies this by writing his reports in a 'feigned hand'. Much of the deceitful talk is concerned with attachments of various kinds and the severing of these. Mrs Clackitt is credited with 'six matches being broken off', 'four forced elopements'. 'close confinements' and 'two divorces'. The conversation continues by dealing with three presumed affairs. Snake imagines that Joseph Surface and Lady Sneerwell are having an intrigue. However, Lady Sneerwell quickly points out that Joseph is not attached to *her*, but to Maria. Here Snake makes another false assumption about the pair, for Joseph has an interest only in Maria's fortune and not in the girl herself. Lady Sneerwell goes on to speak of her own passion for Charles Surface, a passion that has not been returned, and is unlikely to be so as Charles is truly in love with Maria. Thus, in the matter of these three romances, little is as it seems, and onlookers are deceived. Whilst this conversation is in progress Lady Sneerwell is making up her face. This quiet act is in itself a form of deceit, for Lady Sneerwell changes the reality of her face into an artifice. The gap between appearance and reality is stressed when Lady Sneerwell speaks of Joseph Surface. Although he is praised by Peter Teazle as the Man of Sentiment, yet, says Lady Sneerwell, she has 'found him out a long time since', and she goes on to reveal him as 'artful, selfish and malicious.'

The audience is introduced to a third theme running through the play, that of the 'Man of Sentiment'. Sneerwell alludes to Joseph as a 'sentimental knave', and Snake quotes Teazle's belief that Joseph is the 'Man of Sentiment'. Here a paradox is presented as each person uses the term in a different sense. A 'sentimental knave' is a person who makes moral generalisations. Such aphorisms, by their general nature, are hollow, and often reflect the emptiness of the speaker. In contrast a 'Man of Sentiment' is one who reflects with enjoyment on private emotion.

The use of language is one of the means by which the two characters communicate with the audience. Lady Sneerwell is a questioner; in this excerpt we see her delving to get more information from Snake. Many of Lady Sneerwell's sentences are balanced in an artificial binary form - one half of the sentence echoes the other. Thus: 'She certainly has talents, but her *manner* is gross.' This trait emphasises the artificiality of the person. Another characteristic is to take an unpleasant situation and gloss over it with a telling turn of phrase. Thus, an intriguing part of her early life is rapidly passed over: 'Wounded myself in the early part of my life by the envenomed tongue of slander. . .'.

Snake has his own syntactical constructions which highlight the kind of person he is. He makes formal speeches, framing within them long and complicated sentences. Taking up Lady Sneerwell's reference to Sir Peter Teazle's wards, Joseph and Charles Surface, Snake composes a sentence which is not only formulated with balance and precision, but is tightly packed with information:

> . . . here are two young men, to whom Sir Peter has acted as a kind of Guardian since their Father's death, the elder possessing the most amiable Character and universally well spoken of, the other the most dissipated and extravagant young fellow in the Kingdom without Friends or Character - the former an avow'd Admirer of your Ladyship, and apparently your Favourite; the latter attached to Maria, Sir Peter's ward - and confessedly belov'd by her - now on the face of these circumstances it is utterly unaccountable to me why you, the Widow of a City Knight with a good Jointure - should not close with the Passion of a man of such character and expectations as Mr. Surface - and more so why you should be so uncommonly earnest to destroy the mutual Attachment - subsisting between his brother Charles and Maria.

In this instance the effect of the lengthy sentence is to show the audience the pomposity of the character.

In these first eighty lines of the play we see that two characters establish themselves, and they are then used to introduce other characters and the main themes of the plot. That Sheridan achieves this within so brief a span, is an indication of the disciplined economy with which he worked.

# 7 THE CRITICAL RECEPTION

## 7.1 PREPARATIONS

On one occasion Sheridan described his method of composing a play: 'When I have fix'd any characters and the Construction of my Plot, I can go on with the Dialogue, travelling, visiting, walking, anyhow and any-where.' We have already seen (in Section 5.4) that Sheridan based his characters on the actors he knew would perform. We have seen, too, that Sheridan developed in the first instance two strands in the plot of his comedy - that connected with the slanderers and the adventures of the newly-wed, but seemingly incompatible, Teazles. From this point the dialogue was developed and given to certain characters. In his revisions of the text the dialogue was sometimes apportioned to different people, occasionally with an incongruous result. After his work on the foundations of character and possible construction, the text grew slowly, and consid-erable pressure had to be placed on Sheridan to write the parts in time for adequate rehearsal. Much of the worry fell on William Hopkins, the prompter at Drury Lane, whose work resembled that of a modern stage manager. However, at length Sheridan was able to scribble at the end of his manuscript:

> – finis –
> Thank God!
> RBS
> . . .

To this either the playwright, or the prompter, added the heartfelt rejoinder:

> Amen!
> W. Hopkins

The manuscript was submitted to the Lord Chamberlain's office for a licence, that the play might receive public performance on 8 May 1777.

Sheridan was surprised to discover on the day before the performance that this had been refused on the grounds that the portrait of Moses represented a real Jewish moneylender and, more seriously, implicated one William Hopkins (not the prompter), who received large sums of money for obtaining annuities in the process of dealing with usurers. Not to be thwarted, Sheridan went to see the Lord Chamberlain on the following morning, and explained that the scene was a general satire on usury and not aimed at the practice of any specific person. The Lord Chamberlain laughed at the circumstances and lifted his ban. Neither Sheridan's procrastinations, nor the objections of the over-sensitive, could then prevent the staging of *The School for Scandal*.

## 7.2 THE FIRST NIGHT

The Theatre Royal at Drury Lane was crowded. The Duchess of Devonshire headed a list of London society which had arrived to see the piece. From the auditorium the spectators watched on stage a barbed reflection of themselves. Richard Cumberland, as might be expected, found the lack of moral tone in the piece distressing and is alleged to have pinched his over-amused children, saying to them: 'There is nothing to laugh at my little angels.' Most, however, rose in delighted applause. Henry Angelo (1760–1839?), a fashionable fencing master, related that a friend of his passed the theatre and likened the approbation which greeted the fall of the screen in the fourth act to an explosion which might have endangered the safety of the building.

## 7.3 RECEPTION

On the following days the Press described the success of the comedy. Many writers saw Sheridan as the equal of his beloved playwright William Congreve (1670–1729). Since taking over the management of the theatre in the previous year, Sheridan had staged a number of Congreve's comedies from a pre-sentimental era and the revivals had been enjoyed; thus Sheridan, to some extent, prepared his audience for his own play. Typical of these comparisons with the earlier dramatist was the remark which appeared in the *Gazetteer*:

> They who have a sufficient knowledge of literature, will not offer to contest that Congreve sits unrivalled on the throne of dramatic wit; – and if any author has a right to dispute Congreve's royal supremacy, it is the writer of *The School for Scandal*.

The critic of the *London Evening Post* mentioned the wit which sparkled, sometimes to excess, in the comedy. If there was a fault in this, then it was a fault shared with Congreve. This same writer commended Sheridan, too, for subduing, in his writing, 'the Dragon of mere sentimental drama'; the writings of Sheridan and Goldsmith helped to establish a more robust taste for the comedy which induces hearty laughter rather than tears.

Writers selected scenes which, for them, were the highlights of the play. Naturally enough the auction and the screen scenes attracted favourable comment. Of the first, a writer in the *London Magazine* noted that the 'scene is happily imagined, and is rich in sentiment and nature'. 'Nature' is a word often used in eighteenth-century criticism; Sir Joshua Reynolds (1723-92), the founder of the Royal Academy, in his lectures used it to mean an idealised concept of nature. Charles is treating the memory of his uncle with that respect and fondness which an ideally benevolent young man would employ.

In its construction the screen scene gained many plaudits. Not an original device, Sheridan managed it with a consummate skill which drew approval. The *Morning Chronicle* was typical in its remark:

> It is almost the first time we ever saw a screen introduced and a closet used, without exclaiming against the incidents as devices.

For some, the point in the play at which this scene was placed posed a problem; it was thought that the scene should come nearer the termination. A writer commented as late as 1792 in the *Thespian Magazine and Literary Repository*:

> The screen scene being introduced too soon, the plot is discovered in the fourth act - therefore the character of Joseph, that canting, smiling hypocrite. . .is suddenly revealed. - The last act, which should be the best, is consequently the worst.

It is instructive to take the scenes in the fourth and fifth acts of the play and to attempt to reassemble them in a new formation. That few choices were left to Sheridan, and that he dealt skilfully with the problem, rapidly becomes apparent.

The brilliance of the dialogue too was praised. 'The dialogue of this comedy is easy, engaging and witty,' said a writer in the *Morning Chronicle*, and the *Morning Post* echoed the commendation: '. . .the principal excellence of the Comedy will be found in the wit and elegance of the dialogue, with which it abounds.'

There were, of course, a number of minor criticisms, and some of these were shaped by the tastes of the time. For example, sentimental dramatists had dispensed with the subplot in many of their plays so that the full moral impact of the central situation was felt. That *The School for Scandal* contains a number of themes was a matter for concern, and the weaving of these into a single plot did not allay worries about which theme was the principal. Typical is a comment by a critic in the *Morning Chronicle*: '. . .the poet has adopted a double plot, when a single one would not only have been a sufficient groundwork, but, if well conducted, would have been essentially contributory to the roundness and perfection of the piece.' The *London Magazine* felt that the play lacked a central character around whom the main plot revolved; supplying a solution to this problem, the *Morning Chronicle* suggested that the character of Joseph should be amplified and the title of *The Man of Sentiment* given to the piece. This, however, would presumably have been abhorrent to Sheridan as it would entail falling back on the stock formulae of the sentimental dramatists.

The strength of the casting won praise. Sheridan had been told, as he began work on the play, that the resources of the full company of Drury Lane would be his in staging the piece. To enjoy such a spread of talent was a rare privilege. Sir Horace Walpole represents the views of many delighted spectators:

> To my great astonishment there were more parts performed admirably in *The School for Scandal* than I almost ever saw in any play. . . . It seemed a marvellous resurrection of the stage.

Some sentences from William Hazlitt, written in 1819, may serve as a summary of the opinions we have been considering. The unique artistry of Sheridan was singled out:

> *The School for Scandal* is, if not the most original, perhaps the most finished and faultless comedy which we have. When it is acted you hear people all around you exclaiming, 'Surely it is impossible for anything to be cleverer'.

He praised, too, the cleansing effect of the satire:

> Besides the wit and ingenuity of this play, there is a genial spirit of frankness and generosity about it, that relieves the heart as well as clears the lungs.

Sheridan, Hazlitt claimed, believed in a benevolence which underpins the actions of mankind, but he was too much of a realist to write a sentimental comedy about idealised humanity:

> [Sheridan] professes a faith in the natural goodness, as well as natural depravity of human nature. While [he] strips off the mask of hypocrisy, [he] inspires a confidence between man and man.

In spite of minor quibbles, Sheridan's play was obviously, and quite rightly, accepted as a resounding success. Its inclusion in the theatrical repertiore today shows that the play transcends the objectives of Sheridan's satire and the changing social circumstances of the past two hundred years. It is an example of dramatic craftsmanship and a view of human nature which displays permanent qualities.

Yet strangely the piece has attracted little critical attention since Hazlitt wrote his appreciation, and the numerous theatrical revivals have not prompted serious considerations of the text. It is only with the complete edition of Sheridan's works, edited by Cecil Price, that the worth of Sheridan as a playwright has been acknowledged. The intervening dearth is an unfortunate reflection of the dismissive attitude adopted by many scholars towards late-eighteenth-century comedy.

## 7.4 SOME ROLES REVIVED

When a play which has been written for particular performers at a selected London theatre transfers to a company in a provincial theatre a sense of loss may be experienced. In the role of Charles Surface, Smith gave way to John Philip Kemble, a dignified but static actor who excelled in tragedy rather than the comic *genre*. Charles Lamb described his sober performance:

> His harshest tones in this part came steeped and dulcified in good humour. He made his defects a grace. His exact declamatory manner, as he managed it, only served to convey the points of his dialogue with more precision.

If the portrayal of Charles was acceptable, Lamb could no longer find satisfaction when King was replaced in the role of Sir Peter. A new generation of actors was interested in naturalism, and unsuitably brought this to the portrayal of the role:

> . . .Sir Peter Teazle must be no longer the comic idea of a fretful old bachelor bridegroom. . . - he must be a real person, capable in law of sustaining an injury - a person towards whom duties are to be acknowledged - the genuine *crim. con.* antagonist of the villanous seducer Joseph. To realise him more, his sufferings under his unfortunate match must have the downright pungency of life - must (or should) make you not mirthful but uncomfortable, just as the same predicament would move you in a neighbour or old friend.

Changing styles of acting is one of the difficulties which dogs a play in performance, and presentations of *The School for Scandal* suffered from this.

An example of this difficulty can be seen in a personification of Charles Surface by Charles Coghlan (1842-99) at the Prince of Wales Theatre in 1874.

The dramatic critic, Clement Scott (1841-1904) has described the business he introduced in the course of the auction scene:

> How admirable is the touch when Sir Oliver, anxious to become the purchaser of his own picture, the young man kneels on the settee before it and is lost in a reverie of old days and old kindnesses.

The text contains no suggestion that a display of sentimentalism should take place here or anywhere else. It is sufficient for the actor to realise that Sheridan held an optimistic view of human nature.

Sheridan strongly delineates each character, and whilst there is information enough for the performer to work on, the author's artistry allows space enough for a variety of interpretations to be brought to roles without violating the spirit of the play. Mrs Abington was followed in the part of Lady Teazle by Elizabeth Farren (1759-1829), who herself married into an aristocratic family and became the Countess of Derby. She brought qualities of refinement to the role. Dorothy Jordan, the mistress of the Duke of Clarence, took over the part, turning Lady Teazle into a romping girl with an infectious laugh for which she was famous. These are polarities of approach confined within an acceptable spectrum.

The performers of today must still consider carefully the demands of the text in creating a stage character. Beryl Reid took the role of Mrs Candour in a production which played in 1983 at the Theatre Royal, Haymarket and the Duke of York's Theatre. In preparing for the part, she at first found the character unrewarding, but perserving hit upon the idea that Mrs Candour is, in contrast to the other slanderers, too straitened financially to own a carriage and so goes from house to house on foot. She further elaborated this notion in her realisation that many of the houses are set some distance apart and that the cobbled streets will in no time cause problems to the malicious lady's feet. In her book *So Much Love* she described how this idea affected her physical portrayal of the character:

> All the running about made her very rocky on her feet, so she was bent almost double by her exertions in keeping up with the scandal. Once again, the shoes and the walk helped me to find the character. . .

Now whilst this use of one's imagination is an intrinsic part of the performer's creativity, it must be anchored to the text. Lady Sneerwell's servant suggests, immediately prior to Mrs Candour's first entry, that she does not exist in this impoverished and highly ambulatory state: 'Madam, Mrs Candour is below and, if your ladyship's at leisure, will leave her carriage' (1.1).

To sum up: performers taking part in revivals of *The School for Scandal* have found that the text offers strong guidelines on the portrayal of their roles; yet the characters are delineated with creative artistry by the playwright to the extent that, within the textual framework, there is room for a performer to manoeuvre; however, in doing this each actor must be sensitive to the tone of the complete play and responsive to his historical sense of life in Georgian London. This is a discipline which transforms Sheridan's sparkling text into a living work of art.

# REVISION QUESTIONS

1. What do you learn about the nature of satire from *The Scandal for Scandal*?

2. Sheridan's play is a comedy; but wherein lies the humour?

3. What aspects of contemporary London life does Sheridan portray in *The School for Scandal*?

4. What part does disguise and deception play in *The School for Scandal*? Are they related?

5. What is meant by 'the Man of Sentiment'?

6. Comment on the language of the play.

7. Compare the character of Charles Surface with that of his brother Joseph.

8. 'The character of Joseph is but a sketch and a bad one.' So wrote 'Theatrical Critic' in the *St James' Chronicle*. Do you agree with him?

9. What are the basic conflicts which form the dynamism of the plot?

10. Choose a key scene in the play, justify your choice, and comment on the way in which you would direct it.

11. Which role would you prefer to play in *The School for Scandal*? Why? What costume would you wear in order to emphasise your character?

72

12.  Write a review of a production of *The School for Scandal*.

13.  Thomas Moore claimed that the amalgam of the plots of 'The Teazles' and 'The Slanderers' gave 'that excessive opulence of wit, with which, as some critics think, the dialogue is overloaded'. Are you aware of this overloading?

# FURTHER READING

*Works by Richard Brinsley Sheridan*
Cecil Price, ed., *The Dramatic Works of Richard Brinsley Sheridan* (Oxford University Press, 1973). Sheridan's plays complete in two volumes. There is a general introduction, a very full introduction to the individual plays and copious footnotes. This is an invaluable work of reference.
Cecil Price, ed., *Sheridan's Plays* (London: Oxford University Press, 1975). In this single volume paperback is a highly informative general introduction, brief footnoting and the complete plays of Sheridan.
F. W. Bateson, ed., *The School for Scandal* (London: Ernest Benn, New Mermaids, 1979). Bateson gives many interesting details of staging based on a number of Drury Lane prompt books. A highly informative introduction.

*Literary and historical background, criticism and biography*
Bingham, Madeleine, *The Track of a Comet* (London: George Allen & Unwin Ltd, 1972). A biography of the playwright written in an easy but scholarly style. Well illustrated.
Darlington, W. A., *Sheridan* (London: Longmans, Green & Co. for the British Council and the National Book League, 1951). A brief critical biography, which effectively sums up Sheridan's achievements.
Lamb, Charles, *The Art of the Stage as set out in 'Lamb's Dramatic Essays'* (ed. Percy Fitzgerald) (London: Remington & Co., 1885). A compendium of essays giving a picture of the London stage in Georgian times. The essay 'On the Artificial Comedy of The Last Century' contains an appreciation of John Palmer as Joseph Surface.
Loftis, John, *Sheridan and the Drama of Georgian England* (Oxford: Basil Blackwell, 1976). A chapter is devoted to *The School for Scandal*. Loftis views Sheridan as the last of the line of Restoration dramatists. An erudite essay which introduces many new trains of thought.

Novak, Maximillian E., *Eighteenth-Century English Literature* (London: Macmillan, 1983). A clear survey which helps to place Sheridan in a literary context.

Leech, Clifford and Craik, T. W., eds, *The Revels History of Drama in English*, Volume VI: 1750-1880 (London: Methuen, 1975). This illustrated work describes in detail the theatrical conditions prevailing in Sheridan's day. A copious bibliography is given.

Sherbo, Arthur, *English Sentimental Drama* (East Lansing: Michigan State University Press, 1957). A substantial work which helps to clarify the meaning of the phrase 'a Man of Sentiment'.

## Mastering English Literature
### Richard Gill

*Mastering English Literature* will help readers both to enjoy
English Literature and to be successful in 'O' levels, 'A' levels
and other public exams. It is an introduction to the study of
poetry, novels and drama which helps the reader in four ways –
by providing ways of approaching literature, by giving examples
and practice exercises, by offering hints on how to write about
literature, and by the author's own evident enthusiasm for the
subject. With extracts from more than 200 texts, this is an
enjoyable account of how to get the maximum satisfaction out
of reading, whether it be for formal examinations or simply
for pleasure.

## Work Out English Literature ('A' level)
### S.H. Burton

This book familiarises 'A' level English Literature candidates
with every kind of test which they are likely to encounter.
Suggested answers are worked out step by step and accompanied by full author's commentary. The book helps students
to clarify their aims and establish techniques and standards so
that they can make appropriate responses to similar questions
when the examination pressures are on. It opens up fresh ways
of looking at the full range of set texts, authors and critical
judgements and motivates students to know more of these
matters.

# Also from Macmillan

# CASEBOOK SERIES

The Macmillan *Casebook* series brings together the best of modern criticism with a selection of early reviews and comments. Each Casebook charts the development of opinion on a play, poem, or novel, or on a literary genre, from its first appearance to the present day.

## GENERAL THEMES

COMEDY: DEVELOPMENTS IN CRITICISM
D. J. Palmer

DRAMA CRITICISM: DEVELOPMENTS SINCE IBSEN
A. J. Hinchliffe

THE ENGLISH NOVEL: DEVELOPMENTS IN CRITICISM SINCE HENRY JAMES
Stephen Hazell

THE LANGUAGE OF LITERATURE
N. Page

THE PASTORAL MODE
Bryan Loughrey

THE ROMANTIC IMAGINATION
J. S. Hill

TRAGEDY: DEVELOPMENTS IN CRITICISM
R. P. Draper

## POETRY

WILLIAM BLAKE: SONGS OF INNOCENCE AND EXPERIENCE
Margaret Bottrall

BROWNING: MEN AND WOMEN AND OTHER POEMS
J. R. Watson

BYRON: CHILDE HAROLD'S PILGRIMAGE AND DON JUAN
John Jump

CHAUCER: THE CANTERBURY TALES
J. J. Anderson

COLERIDGE: THE ANCIENT MARINER AND OTHER POEMS
A. R. Jones and W. Tydeman

DONNE: SONGS AND SONETS
Julian Lovelock

T. S. ELIOT: FOUR QUARTETS
Bernard Bergonzi

T. S. ELIOT: PRUFROCK, GERONTION, ASH WEDNESDAY AND OTHER POEMS
B. C. Southam

T. S. ELIOT: THE WASTELAND
C. B. Cox and A. J. Hinchliffe

ELIZABETHAN POETRY: LYRICAL AND NARRATIVE
Gerald Hammond

THOMAS HARDY: POEMS
J. Gibson and T. Johnson

GERALD MANLEY HOPKINS: POEMS
Margaret Bottrall

KEATS: ODES
G. S. Fraser

KEATS: THE NARRATIVE POEMS
J. S. Hill

MARVELL: POEMS
Arthur Pollard

THE METAPHYSICAL POETS
Gerald Hammond

MILTON: PARADISE LOST
A. E. Dyson and Julian Lovelock

POETRY OF THE FIRST WORLD WAR
Dominic Hibberd

ALEXANDER POPE: THE RAPE OF THE LOCK
John Dixon Hunt

SHELLEY: SHORTER POEMS & LYRICS
Patrick Swinden

SPENSER: THE FAERIE QUEEN
Peter Bayley

TENNYSON: IN MEMORIAM
John Dixon Hunt

THIRTIES POETS: 'THE AUDEN GROUP'
Ronald Carter

WORDSWORTH: LYRICAL BALLADS
A. R. Jones and W. Tydeman

WORDSWORTH: THE PRELUDE
W. J. Harvey and R. Gravil

W. B. YEATS: POEMS 1919–1935
E. Cullingford

W. B. YEATS: LAST POEMS
Jon Stallworthy

# THE NOVEL AND PROSE

JANE AUSTEN: EMMA
David Lodge

JANE AUSTEN: NORTHANGER ABBEY AND PERSUASION
B. C. Southam

JANE AUSTEN: SENSE AND SENSIBILITY, PRIDE AND PREJUDICE AND MANSFIELD PARK
B. C. Southam

CHARLOTTE BRONTË: JANE EYRE AND VILLETTE
Miriam Allott

EMILY BRONTË: WUTHERING HEIGHTS
Miriam Allott

BUNYAN: THE PILGRIM'S PROGRESS
R. Sharrock

CONRAD: HEART OF DARKNESS, NOSTROMO AND UNDER WESTERN EYES
C. B. Cox

CONRAD: THE SECRET AGENT
Ian Watt

CHARLES DICKENS: BLEAK HOUSE
A. E. Dyson

CHARLES DICKENS: DOMBEY AND SON AND LITTLE DORRITT
Alan Shelston

CHARLES DICKENS: HARD TIMES, GREAT EXPECTATIONS AND OUR MUTUAL FRIEND
N. Page

GEORGE ELIOT: MIDDLEMARCH
Patrick Swinden

GEORGE ELIOT: THE MILL ON THE FLOSS AND SILAS MARNER
R. P. Draper

HENRY FIELDING: TOM JONES
Neil Compton

E. M. FORSTER: A PASSAGE TO INDIA
Malcolm Bradbury

HARDY: THE TRAGIC NOVELS
R. P. Draper

HENRY JAMES: WASHINGTON SQUARE AND THE PORTRAIT OF A LADY
Alan Shelston

JAMES JOYCE: DUBLINERS AND A PORTRAIT OF THE ARTIST AS A YOUNG MAN
Morris Beja

D. H. LAWRENCE: THE RAINBOW AND WOMEN IN LOVE
Colin Clarke

D. H. LAWRENCE: SONS AND LOVERS
Gamini Salgado

SWIFT: GULLIVER'S TRAVELS
Richard Gravil

THACKERAY: VANITY FAIR
Arthur Pollard

TROLLOPE: THE BARSETSHIRE
NOVELS
T. Bareham

VIRGINIA WOOLF: TO THE
LIGHTHOUSE
Morris Beja

## DRAMA

CONGREVE: COMEDIES
Patrick Lyons

T. S. ELIOT: PLAYS
Arnold P. Hinchliffe

JONSON: EVERY MAN IN HIS
HUMOUR AND THE ALCHEMIST
R. V. Holdsworth

JONSON: VOLPONE
J. A. Barish

MARLOWE: DR FAUSTUS
John Jump

MARLOWE: TAMBURLAINE,
EDWARD II AND THE JEW OF
MALTA
John Russell Brown

MEDIEVAL ENGLISH DRAMA
Peter Happé

O'CASEY: JUNO AND THE
PAYCOCK, THE PLOUGH AND THE
STARS AND THE SHADOW OF A
GUNMAN
R. Ayling

JOHN OSBORNE: LOOK BACK IN
ANGER
John Russell Taylor

WEBSTER: THE WHITE DEVIL AND
THE DUCHESS OF MALFI
R. V. Holdsworth

WILDE: COMEDIES
W. Tydeman

## SHAKESPEARE

SHAKESPEARE: ANTONY AND
CLEOPATRA
John Russell Brown

SHAKESPEARE: CORIOLANUS
B. A. Brockman

SHAKESPEARE: HAMLET
John Jump

SHAKESPEARE: HENRY IV PARTS
I AND II
G. K. Hunter

SHAKESPEARE: HENRY V
Michael Quinn

SHAKESPEARE: JULIUS CAESAR
Peter Ure

SHAKESPEARE: KING LEAR
Frank Kermode

SHAKESPEARE: MACBETH
John Wain

SHAKESPEARE: MEASURE FOR
MEASURE
G. K. Stead

SHAKESPEARE: THE MERCHANT
OF VENICE
John Wilders

SHAKESPEARE: A MIDSUMMER
NIGHT'S DREAM
A. W. Price

SHAKESPEARE: MUCH ADO
ABOUT NOTHING AND AS YOU
LIKE IT
John Russell Brown

SHAKESPEARE: OTHELLO
John Wain

SHAKESPEARE: RICHARD II
N. Brooke

SHAKESPEARE: THE SONNETS
Peter Jones

SHAKESPEARE: THE TEMPEST
D. J. Palmer

SHAKESPEARE: TROILUS AND
CRESSIDA
Priscilla Martin

SHAKESPEARE: TWELFTH NIGHT
D. J. Palmer

SHAKESPEARE: THE WINTER'S
TALE
Kenneth Muir

# MACMILLAN SHAKESPEARE VIDEO WORKSHOPS

## DAVID WHITWORTH

Three unique book and video packages, each examining a particular aspect of Shakespeare's work; tragedy, comedy and the Roman plays. Designed for all students of Shakespeare, each package assumes no previous knowledge of the plays and can serve as a useful introduction to Shakespeare for 'O' and 'A' level candidates as well as for students at colleges and institutes of further, higher and adult education.

The material is based on the New Shakespeare Company Workshops at the Roundhouse, adapted and extended for television. By combining the resources of television and a small theatre company, this exploration of Shakespeare's plays offers insights into varied interpretations, presentation, styles of acting as well as useful background information.

While being no substitute for seeing the whole plays in performance, it is envisaged that these video cassettes will impart something of the original excitement of the theatrical experience, and serve as a welcome complement to textual analysis leading to an enriched and broader view of the plays.

Each package consists of:

* the Macmillan Shakespeare editions of the plays concerned;

* a video cassette available in VHS or Beta;

* a leaflet of teacher's notes.


**THE TORTURED MIND**
looks at the four tragedies Hamlet, Othello, Macbeth and King Lear.

**THE COMIC SPIRIT**
examines the comedies Much Ado About Nothing, Twelfth Night, A Midsummer Night's Dream, and As You Like It.

**THE ROMAN PLAYS**
Features Julius Caesar, Antony and Cleopatra
and Coriolanus

# THE MACMILLAN SHAKESPEARE

General Editor: PETER HOLLINDALE
Advisory Editor: PHILIP BROCKBANK

The Macmillan Shakespeare features:
* clear and uncluttered texts with modernised punctuation and spelling wherever possible;
* full explanatory notes printed on the page facing the relevant text for ease of reference;
* stimulating introductions which concentrate on content, dramatic effect, character and imagery, rather than mere dates and sources.

Above all, The Macmillan Shakespeare treats each play as a work for the theatre which can also be enjoyed on the page.

**CORIOLANUS**
Editor: Tony Parr

**THE WINTER'S TALE**
Editor: Christopher Parry

**MUCH ADO ABOUT NOTHING**
Editor: Jan McKeith

**RICHARD II**
Editor: Richard Adams

**RICHARD III**
Editor: Richard Adams

**HENRY IV, PART I**
Editor: Peter Hollindale

**HENRY IV, PART II**
Editor: Tony Parr

**HENRY V**
Editor: Brian Phythian

**AS YOU LIKE IT**
Editor: Peter Hollindale

**A MIDSUMMER NIGHT'S DREAM**
Editor: Norman Sanders

**THE MERCHANT OF VENICE**
Editor: Christopher Parry

**THE TAMING OF THE SHREW**
Editor: Robin Hood

**TWELFTH NIGHT**
Editor: E. A. J. Honigmann

**THE TEMPEST**
Editor: A. C. Spearing

**ROMEO AND JULIET**
Editor: James Gibson

**JULIUS CAESAR**
Editor: D. R. Elloway

**MACBETH**
Editor: D. R. Elloway

**HAMLET**
Editor: Nigel Alexander

**ANTONY AND CLEOPATRA**
Editors: Jan McKeith and
Richard Adams

**OTHELLO**
Editors: Celia Hilton and R. T. Jones

**KING LEAR**
Editor: Philip Edwards

# MACMILLAN STUDENTS' NOVELS

## General Editor: JAMES GIBSON

The Macmillan Students' Novels are low-priced, new editions of major classics, aimed at the first examination candidate. Each volume contains:

*   enough explanation and background material to make the novels accessible − and rewarding    to pupils with little or no previous knowledge of the author or the literary period;

*   detailed notes elucidate matters of vocabulary, interpretation and historical background;

*   eight pages of plates comprising facsimiles of manuscripts and early editions, portraits of the author and photographs of the geographical setting of the novels.

JANE AUSTEN: MANSFIELD PARK
Editor: Richard Wirdnam

JANE AUSTEN: NORTHANGER ABBEY
Editor: Raymond Wilson

JANE AUSTEN: PRIDE AND PREJUDICE
Editor: Raymond Wilson

JANE AUSTEN: SENSE AND SENSIBILITY
Editor: Raymond Wilson

JANE AUSTEN: PERSUASION
Editor: Richard Wirdnam

CHARLOTTE BRONTË: JANE EYRE
Editor: F. B. Pinion

EMILY BRONTË: WUTHERING HEIGHTS
Editor: Graham Handley

JOSEPH CONRAD: LORD JIM
Editor: Peter Hollindale

CHARLES DICKENS: GREAT EXPECTATIONS
Editor: James Gibson

CHARLES DICKENS: HARD TIMES
Editor: James Gibson

CHARLES DICKENS: OLIVER TWIST
Editor: Guy Williams

CHARLES DICKENS: A TALE OF TWO CITIES
Editor: James Gibson

GEORGE ELIOT: SILAS MARNER
Editor: Norman Howlings

GEORGE ELIOT: THE MILL ON THE FLOSS
Editor: Graham Handley

D. H. LAWRENCE: SONS AND LOVERS
Editor: James Gibson

D. H. LAWRENCE: THE RAINBOW
Editor: James Gibson

MARK TWAIN: HUCKLEBERRY FINN
Editor: Christopher Parry